Inverness, February, 1984.

Jacqueline du Pré

IMPRESSIONS

Jacqueline du Pré

IMPRESSIONS

Edited by
WILLIAM WORDSWORTH

Foreword by
HRH THE PRINCE OF WALES

GRANADA
London Toronto Sydney New York

Granada Publishing Limited
8 Grafton Street, London W1X 3LA

Published by Granada Publishing 1983
Reprinted 1983
Copyright © Granada Publishing 1983

British Library Cataloguing in Publication Data

Jacqueline du Pré,
1. Du Pré, Jacqueline   2. Violinists,
violoncellists, etc.—Great Britain—Biography
I. Wordsworth, William
787'.3'0924   ML418.D/

ISBN 0–246–11321–9

Phototypeset by Wyvern Typesetting Ltd, Bristol
Printed in Great Britain by Mackays of Chatham Ltd

Whate'er the theme, the Maiden sang
As if her song could have no ending;
I saw her singing at her work,
And o'er the sickle bending;
I listened, motionless and still;
And, as I mounted up the hill,
The music in my heart I bore,
Long after it was heard no more. *

*When Jacqueline du Pré received a doctorate from HM Queen Elizabeth, the Queen Mother, then Chancellor of London University, Professor John Barron read the oration which he concluded with the last verse of 'The Solitary Reaper' by the poet William Wordsworth

Foreword

by

HRH THE PRINCE OF WALES

I was surprised and flattered to have been asked to write the foreword to this book about Jacqueline du Pré and I am writing it as someone who admires her very deeply – both as a musician and as a person. I shall never forget the first time I saw her perform in the Festival Hall when she played the Haydn C major Cello Concerto. I know that her mother says I saw her perform in a children's television concert when I was about ten years old, but I regret to say that I simply cannot remember anything about it! The Festival Hall concert was a revelation for me. Suddenly the cello took on a new significance in my experience. I was positively electrified, and deeply moved, by the way in which she extracted such magical sounds from the instrument and my memory of the evening is dominated by a pretty girl with a powerful personality and with unbelievably long, blonde hair which flew about her shoulders as she put her heart and soul into the music.

As a result of that memorable evening I became fascinated by the prospect of trying to learn the cello in my last year or two at school. Although I really was very mediocre in my ability, playing the cello gave me immense satisfaction and pleasure – both at school and university. There is nothing quite like the joy of making music with other people, whether it be in an orchestra, a quartet or in a jazz group and I shall always be thoroughly indebted to Jacqueline du Pré for arousing my interest in an instrument which is by no means easy to play!

I have met Jacqueline du Pré on numerous occasions since I saw her in the Festival Hall. It is always great fun when she appears since her sense of humour is infectious and she has a wonderful ability to giggle uncontrollably. The real tragedy, of course, is that we can no longer hear her produce exquisite music. If it is a tragedy for us, what can it be for her? It is very nearly impossible to comprehend why such a thing should happen to someone so uniquely talented, so young and with so much future potential. I have often tried to imagine what it must be like for her – the sense of desperate frustration and impotence when you have so much inside you (God's gift), which you long to impart to others, but which is prevented by a physical barrier. Human existence on this earth is plagued by a never-ending succession of such incomprehensible, and sometimes almost intolerable, occurrences which seem to be designed as some kind of inequitable endurance test. Perhaps, however, one day the scales will be lifted from our eyes and these mysteries will be revealed to us.

Jacqueline du Pré is a courageous individual with a generous and affectionate spirit and many more people, better qualified to judge, who have contributed to this book will attest to that. Their contributions show what an effect she has had on so many people throughout her life so far.

Contents

Acknowledgements

The Editor thanks all those who have provided this affectionate collection of tributes and the Barenboims' many friends who always willingly gave of their time to talk with him. He is greatly indebted to Mrs Derek du Pré for letting us reproduce family photographs and other illustrations. He also thanks Roger Schlesinger, until recently of Granada Publishing, and Anne Charvet, a senior editor at Granada, for their enthusiastic help and encouragement.

Thanks are also due to all those who have kindly given permission to reproduce copyright passages and photographs. Sources of extracts and photographs are given in the appropriate places.

Introduction

'Nobody can write the life of a man but those who have eaten and drunk and lived in social intercourse with him.' So said Samuel Johnson according to his biographer James Boswell. Here then the good doctor's definition of those qualified to subscribe to biography is fulfilled most precisely. That the remark was made by the great lexicographer will give particular pleasure to the subject of this book. A recent gift from her husband, Daniel Barenboim, was a large and splendidly bound volume of the famous English dictionary which Dr Johnson spent eight years compiling.

Unable to express herself through music, Jacqueline du Pré has discovered a great fascination in words and with it developed a talent for writing to convey her feelings. A few brief examples are included later in the book.

Amusing, witty and extremely good company, Jackie always displays an incredibly impressive attitude of strength and determination to live life uncomplainingly and as fully as possible. Quick to reject insincerity and humbug, yet appreciative and compassionate, she has a most resilient nature and is rarely depressed; at least not when she has friends around her.

Many moments occur when her irrepressible sense of mischief and fun have to assert themselves. In sharp contrast are her serious periods of deeply concentrated thought and determination to overcome problems, together with a remarkably spontaneous feeling for life; these are some of the things that contributed to her brilliance as a musician. In his extremely entertaining book about music festivals, *Conducted Tour*, Bernard Levin refers to 'that group of younger musicians . . . who give the appearance of making music for fun. They attend each other's concerts, which is a clue; the fun is shared.' Jackie was one of that group.

When I began to collect contributions from Jackie's colleagues I was warned that it was likely to take longer than I imagined. It was certainly not that the contributors were reluctant to cooperate, simply that sometimes it was not always easy to establish contact as some of them make such mercurial movements around the world. Regrettably it was not possible to include a contribution from Artur Rubinstein although he had expressed a wish to provide one.

Talking with so many of the Barenboims' friends I soon realized how extremely affectionately they are both regarded. Two of their actor friends, Joanna David and Edward Fox, told me of their first meeting with Jackie, when she joined with other actor friends at Upottery to read some of her favourite poetry, during the festival held in the tiny Devonshire village in 1980. Moray Welsh, a fellow cellist, recalled his visits to Jackie's concerts during his student days, how he managed to get to know her and eventually became a friend.

The violinist and orchestra leader, Rodney Friend, told me a sadly amusing tale of good intentions. He and his wife, Cynthia, have been close companions of the Barenboims for many years. The story was about the traumatic occasion when the business of buying a wheelchair for Jackie finally had to be faced. Knowing it was going to be no easy undertaking for Daniel Barenboim, Rodney Friend offered to go with him. There were ghastly moments in the shop as they slowly realized all the attendant implications. Somehow the transaction was concluded and they found themselves in the street with the wheelchair. To lighten the emotional strain they applied themselves to the rather ludicrous problem of how best to transport the object to Rodney Friend's car, which was in a multi-storey car park some three hundred yards away.

'Two men pushing an empty wheelchair along a busy London street tend to be a rather curious spectacle,' Rodney Friend explained. 'So we decided Daniel would sit in the wheelchair and I would push.

'All was well until we reached a roadside kerb, which I had no idea how to negotiate. I could see that to push the chair down it I would tip Daniel out and, with my brief experience, I had not yet concluded that I must make the descent backwards. Seeing my dilemma, a kindly man approached us and solved the problem and "invalid and chairperson" went on their way convulsed with hysterical laughter.

'On arrival at the carpark lift, Daniel was just about to jump out of the chair when the kindly man who had previously assisted us appeared again. I put my hands on Daniel's shoulders to indicate he must stay seated and all three of us travelled up together to the eighth floor. By now "invalid and chairperson" were shaking with ill-disguised laughter as I carefully assisted Daniel into my car under the baleful gaze of the kindly man.'

All of which seems to indicate that once being committed to such a situation, there is little to be done except to continue on with it to the end.

This small group of constantly attentive friends also includes the cellist, Joanna Milholland, and her husband, Jose-Luis Garcia, leader of the English Chamber Orchestra, with whom Daniel Barenboim recorded all the Mozart piano concertos and made his opera-conducting début at the 1973 Edinburgh Festival.

The quite extraordinarily devoted care and consideration of Daniel Barenboim for his wife has been mentioned to me by practically everyone who knows him. The strain of such a situation for someone with a heavy schedule of international concert engagements is something that can hardly be imagined. Since the start of Jackie's illness, few days have passed without her having a telephone call from her husband and he so arranges his commitments that, at most times, scarcely two weeks go by without him returning to London, however brief the visit may have to be.

A dedicated band of people have devoted themselves to helping Jackie live her life as normally as possible. In the early days of her illness, Olga, a wonderful Czechoslovakian housekeeper looked after her needs and ran the household. Aida Barenboim, her mother-in-law, makes periodical trips from Israel to help with the supervision of domestic arrangements whenever it becomes necessary as a result of holidays or illness of any members of the resident team.

For some years now, Ruth Anna Cannings, who comes from Guyana, has been Jackie's nurse, companion and friend, caring for her and going with her to most of the numerous concerts and on the other outings to which Jackie looks forward so eagerly. Jackie first met Ruth Anna in 1973 when she became ill and returned from America to go into the Lindo wing of St Mary's Hospital in London for a month. Ruth Ann, as she is generally known, was one of the nurses assigned to her.

Three years later, during the City of London Festival of 1976, Daniel Barenboim was conducting the Beethoven 'Choral' Symphony in St Paul's Cathedral and Ruth Ann, always a music lover, decided to go to the performance. As she was leaving she saw Jackie and they talked for a few moments. Making her way to a bus stop, Ruth Ann was surprised to be overtaken by Aida Barenboim, who asked her if she would consider nursing Jackie. Never having thought of undertaking private nursing and with plans to return to New York, where her parents live, she asked for a little time to think over the proposal. After giving careful consideration to the restrictions that such a job would impose by contrast with hospital work, she finally agreed. A deeply religious person, Ruth Ann has a steadfast belief that it was ordained that she should 'have the privilege of caring for Jackie'.

With her doctors Jackie has a remarkable rapport; they are all good chums together and, as she herself says, she loves them. Whenever their duties allow, they will accompany her to a concert or some social occasion.

With Jackie's physician, Dr Leonard Selby, a great friend of mine, I first discussed the idea of compiling this book, and I would like to thank him for his considerable help, encouragement and guidance.

Dr Leo Lange, who is Jackie's consultant neurologist, has kindly given me a brief description of the symptoms and effects of multiple sclerosis. As so little is generally known about the illness, I thought that his notes should be included here:

> The central nervous system functions as a means of transmitting impulses from one part of the body to another. There are millions of nerve fibres and each is individually insulated. In multiple sclerosis, the sheaths of individual nerves are damaged and this causes various disabilities.
>
> It may affect vision, causing blurring of vision or giving double vision. In later stages of the disease it may cause permanent disability, but in the initial stages usually not. It may affect different parts of the nervous system and may give rise to weakness of the limbs and difficulty in controlling the natural functions, such as the bowels and the water works. It can paralyse one limb, or any number, sometimes producing paralysis of both legs, rarely producing paralysis of arms and legs. Of course, these disabilities do not start abruptly and all together. Many people have a few attacks during their lifetime but may recover virtually completely and their lives are not impaired in any way. At the other end of the scale, there are patients who may have increasingly severe attacks over a matter of

months, or more usually years, and may become severely disabled quite rapidly.

MS is totally unpredictable. You can have a series of attacks, from which you may recover almost completely, depending on how well the sheaths which protect the particular nerves heal themselves; this retreat of the disease is termed a 'remission'. The previous symptoms may never recur, but if they do you cannot tell in advance what part of the nervous system is going to be attacked next, or how badly, or when the attack will come. This unpredictability is one of the most frightening aspects.

Although in itself it is not terminal, severe MS will almost certainly shorten the life-span, because of the secondary complications that arise. For instance, if the legs and sphincters are paralysed, one may get infections in the kidneys that may lead to death, or if the whole body is severely paralysed, one may develop bed sores and chest infections and these may lead to premature death. But less severe MS as a rule does not shorten the life-span, and patients, if they're well looked after, may go on for many years with quite severe disability.

Recent research seems to indicate quite strongly that there is an environmental trigger for MS which may be viral. In addition to that, there is probably a constitutional-immunity factor, as it may well be that we have all been infected by the virus and only those with the appropriate genetic make-up develop the full disease. If this is confirmed and this may take several more years of research, it is reasonable to expect that one might be able to develop a vaccine and possibly vaccinate people against the possibility of developing the disease.

If this treatment is effective one might improve many patients who have the established condition and reduce their disability, although if there has been permanent nerve damage, it is unlikely that complete recovery will take place.

We tried for some time to keep the prospect of this book a secret so that it would be a surprise for Jackie, but somehow she learned what was afoot and one day confronted me with a direct question. 'Well,' she said, 'please don't just use my first name, in solitary isolation, as the title, otherwise people are bound to think it's about a Paris street-walker.' There has been full regard for this injunction and I hope, dear Jackie, that you will like the contents. It is but a small tribute to a remarkable person and will, I think, cause some outbursts of what you describe as your other complaint – 'giggleitis'.

W.W.

Born for the Cello
by
MRS DEREK DU PRÉ

Jackie could sing in tune before she could talk. One day after her bath I was drying her on my lap and I started to sing 'Baa, Baa, Black Sheep'; she began to sing with me – just the tune. After a short while I stopped singing but she continued right through to the end.

Jackie, our younger daughter, was born at Oxford on 26 January 1945. As her father was a member of the Senior Common Room of Worcester College, the Provost gave permission for the christening to be held in the college chapel. Her godparents included Mrs Theodore Holland, wife of the composer – then professor of composition at the Royal Academy of Music – and Lord Lascelles (now Lord Harewood), who was a fellow cadet at Purbright with Jackie's father.

My other recollection from those early years of her musical abilities was when she was about three or four. It was at Christmas time and quite unexpectedly she said she would like to sing 'Away in a Manger'. So she duly stood up and sang it quite perfectly. I was very conscious that there was a great deal more to it than just a little girl singing. There was a special quality about it, quite devoid of the slightest precociousness. It was a perfectly rounded little 'performance'.

The whole of our family have their musical interests. Our eldest daughter, Hilary, is a professional flautist and teaches. Piers, our son, is an airline pilot and a keen singer although, admittedly, only as a hobby.

Jackie's choice of the cello as an instrument was firmly established one afternoon when we were listening to various instruments being demonstrated in a Children's Hour programme. As soon as she heard the cello she said: 'Mummy, that's the sound I want to make.'

The first time she actually grasped a cello to play was when she was four. Mrs Garfield Howe, who was the pianist Denis Matthews's mother-in-law, came down to our home when we were living in Purley, Surrey, to instruct a small class of local children and brought with her a cello for Jackie to play. When I said to her afterwards: 'Jackie, good, that was very nice', she was absolutely enraptured.

'Oh, mummy,' she replied, 'I do so love my cello.' She said this with such a wealth of feeling, or so it seemed to me at the time, that I remember I started seriously speculating to myself about the future. For the following three months Mrs Garfield Howe continued coming each Saturday and it soon became obvious that Jackie was improving rapidly, far more quickly than any of the other children; her progress was quite phenomenal.

Jackie at eight months

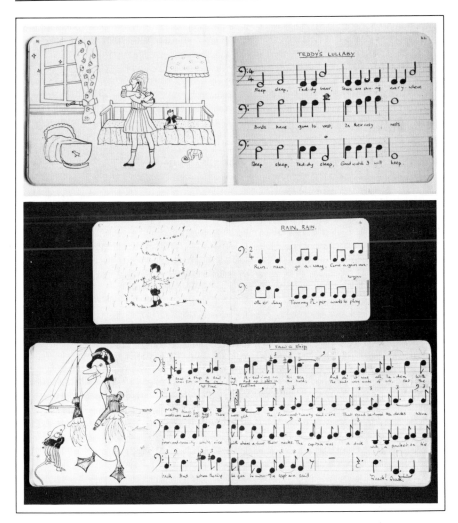

Two of Mrs du Pré's illustrated compositions for Jackie

It was about that time that I began to write little pieces of music for her, pieces suitable for someone of her age and ability. I illustrated them with small sketches around the sides and slipped them under her pillow while she slept. In the morning she would waken early, leap out of bed to get her cello and play the latest composition, before even bothering to get dressed.

Her father and I were a little concerned about what next was best to do with her, as it was clearly apparent that she not only wanted but needed individual tuition. The dilemma was eventually solved by her godmother, Mrs Theodore Holland, who knew Mr Whalen, then running the London Cello School. It was accordingly arranged for Jackie, then aged five, to give an audition for Mr Whalen. He was extremely impressed and at once suggested she have lessons with Alison Dalrymple, who taught at the school and had a great reputation for being good with children. On our way to her lessons, we would call in at a near-by café for an ice-cream or a cold drink. That was really the big moment of the day, because at the café there was a chef with a tall hat, and tall hats of every type had always held a great fascination for Jackie.

After her lesson she would usually go to see Mr Whalen and sit on his knee for a short chat. On one such occasion she interrupted the conversation by putting her head on one side and listening intently

Aged three

to the chimes of the grandfather clock in his office. After a moment or two she said: 'Do you know that that clock is out of tune?' She has always had the most amazingly good ear. After Jackie had been having lessons for about three years at the London Cello School, sadly, Mr Whalen died. It was anyway time for her to move on to another teacher and it was agreed that she should go to William Pleeth. She was supremely happy with him both as a teacher and a friend. He has a rare gift as a teacher; he is not merely a good instructor, he has the outstanding ability to coax from his pupils their latent potentialities. Under his gentle guidance Jackie developed apace.

When, aged ten, she competed for the Suggia Gift she was by far the youngest of the competitors and was in fact the first ever to receive this award. Her winning it meant that her lessons were paid

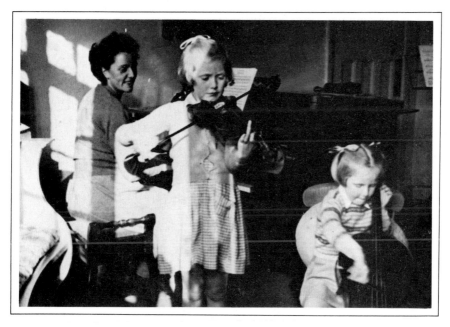

Jackie, aged five, practising with her mother and sister Hilary,
aged seven

for and all manner of wonderful things were done for us; Jackie and I
– she was too young to go alone – were sent one summer to Zermatt,
where she had lessons with Casals. He, of course, had not heard of
her. It was a summer school and each pupil played for him in turn.

After Jackie had played, he said to her: 'Are you English? No, of
course you are not.'

And she replied: 'Yes I am.'

Then he asked her: 'What is your name?'

When she told him he roared with laughter, being fully convinced
that she could not possibly be English if she had such a name (her
father's family is from the Channel Islands) and played with such
uninhibited feeling and intensity. It was, I recall, a memorable
moment, for the great cellist was clearly very deeply impressed with
her vital performance. She admitted to being rather 'bolshie' with
Casals because she was so proud of her own teacher William Pleeth
and was rather unreasonably reluctant to accept things Casals was
trying to convey to her.

We always kept a firm restraint on our younger daughter as far as
public performance was concerned. We were absolutely determined
that in no way would her talent be forced or prematurely exploited.

Early concentration

However, she did make what was her first real public appearance when she played the first movement of the Lalo concerto on television at the age of twelve. Not long after that she returned to the television studio to play the first movement of another concerto, which was the Haydn D major.

When, after a competitive festival in London, a concert was given by the prizewinner, at which Princess Marie Louise presented the prizes, I recollect very clearly that we had a disappointed and rather dejected daughter to cope with because the Princess was not wearing a crown.

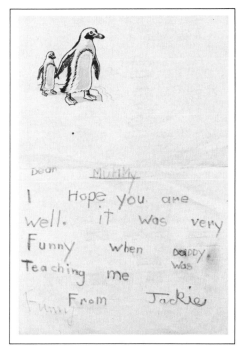

Early recognition of fun

Her first real concert-hall appearance was a recital at the Wigmore Hall in 1961 when she was sixteen, although she had previously played at the Sir Robert Mayer children's concerts.

There was, I believe, at one time, some talk of Jackie giving cello lessons to the Prince of Wales, who has shown a keen interest in the instrument. I can remember the Prince sitting in front of us at the Royal Festival Hall, during a performance of the Haydn C major Cello Concerto. I was told at the time that he was too shy to go round to see Jackie afterwards but, of course, I have no idea if that

Pupils of the London Cello School, 1951; Jackie is seated, second from left

was true. They had met, though, some years before, after a children's television concert in which Jackie played. Prince Charles would have been about ten. He was most interested and afterwards asked if he might examine the cello. Jackie happily agreed. But when the Prince got astride the instrument and started to ride it like a hobbyhorse she became absolutely furious, saying very angrily: 'Please don't treat my cello like that.' Another encounter with the Prince was at St George's Chapel, Windsor, when Jackie and her husband Danny gave a recital which he attended. That meeting was enthusiastic if a little less exuberant. They all three talked happily together afterwards.

Between the ages of sixteen and eighteen Jackie won most of the available musical prizes and awards. But after her first batch of concert appearances and the excitement of them she became greatly depressed, mainly because she would then accept only a few engagements and she seemed to be developing doubts about her ability. It became imperative for her to find something else to do. As if to create some yardstick, she took up all sorts of activities. She painted, she fenced, she did yoga; all manner of things were embraced in her efforts to overcome her frustration. It was not until a long time later that one felt she had finally come to terms with herself and made the decision to become a really good cellist. All this was possibly the metamorphosis of teenager to adult and one must accept that she doubtless felt a little bit lost, particularly after so much early success. Everything seemed to be resolved for her when she went to Dartington for Master Classes with Paul Tortelier, and afterwards to Paris for private tuition with him. Later she went to Moscow for lessons with Rostropovich. She told us that her studies with her three brilliant masters of the cello were, as one would expect, not only exciting but completely fascinating, although she has always considered Pleeth her real mentor and what she liked to call her 'cello daddy'.

She first became really busy when she returned from the Tortelier Master Classes. This was her first taste of travelling abroad alone and she thoroughly enjoyed the experience. In 1965 she toured America with the BBC Symphony Orchestra which was also there for the first time, winning a new and enthusiastic audience for the Elgar Concerto. She had a ten-minute standing ovation in New York. She recorded the concerto with Barbirolli and later on, again in America, with her husband, and she took it to Russia.

Jackie was in Israel with Danny giving concerts and recitals in 1967 during the Six-Day War. She rang up one Monday and said: 'We're getting married on Thursday, can you come?' It was not all that easy as planes were not running to regular schedule, owing to the war. Anyway her father, her brother and I finally arrived after making three changes, rather less than twenty-four hours before the wedding.

The ceremony took place in the old part of the City of Jerusalem, in the house of a rabbi very near the wall. It was rather like a scene from the Old Testament. A large table was in the centre of the room around which the men sat. The women, as is customary, were obliged to sit back around the perimeter of the room. It was a charming and fully traditional ceremony, children and chickens wandered around, as the front door of the house was open to the street. Afterwards there was a special lunch at the King David Hotel and amongst the guests were Ben-Gurion, General Moshe Dayan, Dame Janet Baker and Sir John Barbirolli. In the evening Sir John was conducting Beethoven's Choral Symphony, with Dame Janet as

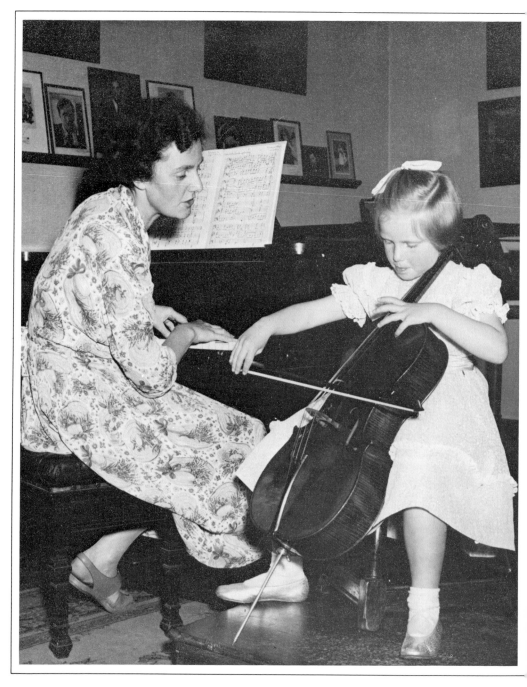

Jackie, aged six, rehearsing with her mother for a concert at the London Cello School

one of the soloists, in celebration of the Israeli victory. In proposing the toast Sir John made a most delightfully amusing speech and was obviously excessively happy. It was a most emotive occasion and a treasured memory.

The fact that Jackie cannot play is, of course, a great loss and sadly frustrating for her. But she continues to have her absorbing interest in music and to participate in the enjoyment and interpretation of the music-making of others. Her television Master Classes were so successful that they were screened a second time. Recording them not only gave her great pleasure, but a really profound sense of satisfaction in being able to pass on some of her knowledge and experience to others.

She has the pleasure, too, of occasionally returning to the concert platform with an orchestra to do readings, as with *Peter and the Wolf*. She also enjoys going to concerts as well as listening to recordings. Some of her own early recordings of various short pieces have recently been released.

There is another extremely comforting and tremendously important aspect of her life: she is fortunate in having a marvellous and devoted husband. With his tightly packed schedule of engagements he never fails regularly to set time aside to devote to her. Considering how much he is obliged to be abroad this is no easy matter. In spite of life's ills, Jackie is happily well aware and most appreciative of its comforting compensations.

My Goddaughter

by

THE EARL OF HAREWOOD

When I came back from the war in May 1945, one of the first people I heard from was Derek du Pré who told me he had a few months before had a daughter and asked if I would be a godfather. Derek and I had become friends when on an Officer Cadets Training Unit course in 1942, a rather dreary period relieved only by the expeditions one could make with friends. He and I used to bicycle over to Aldershot where his wife was in hospital, having just presented him with their first child, Hilary.

It was not until autumn 1945 that Jacqueline was christened and I went to Oxford for the occasion, agreeing with Derek that it was a moot point whether any of the godparents was in a position to support her at the font or whether the rapidly-growing child might not do it better herself.

I saw Jackie only intermittently as she grew up but news of her prowess as a cellist (her mother is a talented musician) was noised abroad, not least by Yehudi Menuhin, and I heard that she was keen to study with the great Russian cellist, Mstislav Rostropovich, whom I knew fairly well. Jackie and her mother came to the house where I then lived and played a Beethoven sonata to Slava's evident satisfaction. He sat down opposite her and made her imitate progressively more difficult exercises and figurations until she had reached the end of her technique. But a little later she went as one of his pupils to Moscow.

She played once at the Edinburgh Festival while I was there and in the late 1960s was quickly accepted as one of the best string players – the best? – England had ever produced. The prodigious talent was not only unmistakable but irresistible, and the tremendous physical energy, which no watcher could miss, was in no sense a cover-up for a lack of it in her approach to the music nor did it contradict a wonderful smoothness and richness of tone in lyric passages. While I worked with the New Philharmonia Orchestra, I remember a not-so-successful performance of the Brahms Double Concerto with Giulini conducting, but that it was followed only a few days later by a performance of the Elgar Cello Concerto which was such stuff as dreams are made on.

Jackie was always in demand as a soloist and after she and Daniel Barenboim were married I used sometimes to visit them to fix up rehearsal details with one or other. I went to their flat early one evening to find Jackie with immense good humour throwing things together before rushing off to play in Paris. She kept the car waiting worryingly long but in the end dashed off confident she would make the plane. Daniel and I had more or less finished an hour or so later when she rang up to say she had missed the plane but would still

Aged eight

The whole family on holiday in Jersey, 1954, L to R: *Jackie, Iris, Piers, Derek and Hilary*

catch the last one of the day. It's not the helter-skelter life that impressed me so much, rather the enviable insouciance with which it was conducted.

My efforts as a godfather have come rather later than is usual, when Jackie could no longer play. So much has been written and said about her courage in adversity that it would be trite to add further words to the mountains which already exist. But certain aspects of her performing personality seem vividly apparent to this day. Her sense of fun, which must have made musical collaboration with her a total joy, is unabated; Jackie's bubbling laughter is familiar to anyone who sees her now. What may perhaps have been less evident in her playing days is the concern she has shown for other cellists, evident not least in the Master Classes she undertook a few years back for the BBC. She showed more than a talent for teaching; this was a true communicator at work on the material she understood best: human beings and music.

I suppose the only piece of luck she has had since 1970 has been hearing music which had not come her way before. I have been with her at the Coliseum at opera or ballet when it has been a privilege to share her joy in music she was meeting for the first time. Records not only give her pleasure but allow anyone with her to witness the sheer concentration and involvement she brings to *listening.*

Whether the music is of central importance or no more than an encore piece, she hears it as if it would fade without her effort, and, when one of her own recordings is on, that seamless 'legato' and rare, even tone seem to come almost as much now from this great listener as it did then from that great cellist.

Pupil Extraordinary
by
WILLIAM PLEETH

It was over twenty-five years ago that the child Jacqueline du Pré came to my house with her mother for her first cello lesson with me. In the previous year her name had been mentioned to me by a young lady of the Hampstead Choir – a Miss White – who chanced to hear Jacqueline and made the prediction that the child would almost certainly be coming to study with me one day. Some months later that prediction came true.

I shall never forget my first meeting with this ten-year-old child, who radiated a lovely sort of innocence, and played to me with complete lack of pretension. It was decided that we would work together, but the extraordinary thing was that, whilst I was immediately aware of a tremendous underlying talent, I didn't as yet realize what a powerfully explosive emotional force I had to deal with. The speed at which she could progress was so rapid that it was like trying to keep pace with a good thoroughbred horse that must be given its head. For instance, I vividly recall how, when she was thirteen, she came for her lesson one Wednesday, and I said: 'Well now, Jackie, we're going to start the Elgar Concerto, and one of the Piatti Caprices. So you'll get the book of Caprices, which are, of course, fiendishly difficult, and we'll start sketching one on Saturday.' Well, lo and behold, this child turned up on the following Saturday, sat down and gave a really fine performance, from memory, of the first movement of the Elgar; and then the first Piatti Caprice, which is extremely difficult, very fast, and two pages long, also from memory. And both very nearly impeccably performed!

When Jackie first played to me, I was struck by one quality in

Piers, Hilary and Jackie, 1955, the day before Hilary played the piano in the BBC programme All Your Own

particular, which is a rather unusual feature in very talented children – a complete lack of precociousness. In many cases early talent is accompanied by external signs, as though the children had an instinctive knowledge of their own abilities – occasionally they are aided unwittingly by parents – resulting in a certain amount of precocious confidence. But in the case of Jackie, the converse could not have been more pronounced.

She had a simple, calm confidence which was brought about by her complete involvement in the music she was playing, and was matched by a concentration of purpose most rare in any child. Even as the need became apparent for opening up a wider field for her study programme, this quality remained intact throughout the years. It was a quality on to which one could graft her other remarkable gifts, and which, in later years, was to make her performances so compelling.

On some of the occasions when my wife and I have visited her during the last two or three years, Jackie and I have indulged in a few minutes of playing cello duets together. So strong is this quality, that one's hearing of what is coming from her instrument soon becomes submerged in the spiritual quality that takes over – something that cuts right through the notes she is trying to play, and emerges as a moving force of great feeling. And this reminds me of another of her indomitable qualities – her humour!

On the first occasion following the onset of her illness that Jackie decided to 'have a go' with our cellos, the telephone conversation went something like this: '. . . and please,' she said, 'can you bring your cello? It will be an awful noise, and my bow will keep slipping over the other side of the bridge, but we can cross that bridge when we come to it!' What a courageous approach and remarkable sense of humour!

It would be impossible for me to capture so many years of study together in so few pages. She was never one of those machinelike fanatics about practising, and it was easy for me to encourage the courageous aspect of music-making – the very heart of spontaneous performance, which made her so exciting to listen to, totally devoid of the still-born qualities so often met with in some performers.

The excitement of making demands on her talents, and her ability to respond to these demands, made for an endless feeding and re-feeding that had the action of a pendulum – or a continuous series of brilliant volleys on Wimbledon's Centre Court. However, there always remained this quiet external calm of her 'outer' person – the

Some very early certificates and awards

outer shell never giving way to great dynamic 'inner' growth – a force which she brought to her playing very early in her victory at the Queen's Prize Competition, and, again, a year later at her remarkable début at Wigmore Hall. As we continued our work, not surprisingly, the demand for her playing began to gather momentum from the concert-giving world.

Everyone is aware of the dangers that lie in the path of such rapid conquests. I myself often pondered as to when Jacqueline should take a few months' break from concerts for the vitally important task of assessing and reassessing the direction in which her career was moving. But it is almost as though some secret agent knew what lay ahead, and brought about a concert timetable of long duration, condensed into a small time-span, thereby enriching the lives of so many people. And for this we, and future generations of music lovers, must feel eternally grateful and privileged.

Jackie's first pupil, Anthony Pleeth, watched by William Pleeth, 1959

Reviews of Jackie's Début
at
WIGMORE HALL ON 1 MARCH 1961

Over the past few weeks London musical audiences have heard several promising and more or less young recitalists. Of these Miss Jacqueline du Pré, who played the cello at Wigmore Hall last night, is but sixteen years old, and yet to speak of promise when reviewing her performance would seem almost insulting, for she has attained a mastery of her instrument that is astonishing in one so young.

The long programme seemed to tax her not one whit. Even a recalcitrant A string which forced her to make a second beginning to Handel's G minor Sonata at the start of her recital, could neither unseat the conviction of her interpretations nor disturb her technical control for an instant. After Handel she tackled the E minor Sonata of Brahms and gave it warmth and breadth in the first movement, an enchanting grace in the second and a vivacious intensity in the last that entirely dispelled the workaday gruffness of much of its counterpoint. Debussy's mercurial Sonata was equally well done, and after the interval Miss du Pré presented an account of Bach's C minor unaccompanied Suite that thrilled the blood with its depth and intuitive eloquence. She ended her programme to good effect by displaying her technique and the complete range of tone colours that she and her Stradivarius can command in a transcription of Falla's *Suite Populaire Espagnole*.

The Times

A tribute from Pablo Casals, Zermatt 1960

In Jacqueline du Pré, just sixteen, who gave her first Wigmore Hall recital last night, England has a cellist bound, in my opinion, to become a world-beater.

She has a prodigious talent. I reckon that already she is of virtuosic rank.

It was astonishing to listen to the sound that issued from her nut-brown Strad, sound enchanting, spontaneous and marvellously organized, thrilling in its emotional range.

The maturity of this child's performance was, indeed, almost incredible.

Jacqueline was born to play the cello. She thoroughly understands its genius, and so instinctive is her reaction to the music that one feels the subtlest ideas of the composer to be embraced.

She is in love with the cello. She sways it with her in each work. Her feelings – serious, stern, proud, triumphant – are shown in her movements and in her face.

With rich and burnished tone, decisive bow-strokes, dramatic pizzicato power, with keen articulation, fire, gentleness, the most delicate shading, she played Handel's G minor Sonata, the Brahms

Sonata in E minor, Debussy's D minor Sonata, and the Bach unaccompanied Suite No. 5.

What we saw and heard from this schoolgirlish artist was cello mastery.

Percy Cater, *Daily Mail*

It is not often that the 'house full' notice is needed at Wigmore Hall, but it was on Wednesday for the recital by Jacqueline du Pré. She is that rarity, an infant prodigy of the cello, and rarer still in that at the age of sixteen she is already well on the way to a place in the top flight of cellists. At present her playing is rather impassive in its quiet mastery. The pleasure it gives is purely and 'classically' musical, and the beauty of her phrasing is in its poise, its perfect control of rhythm and tone, its purity of sound, rather than in any extra-musical or supra-musical expressiveness. The dexterity of her fingers and bowing wrist in the quick figurations of Handel's G minor Sonata had us gasping with the same sort of admiration as for a bass or a baritone who executes with ease coloratura passages that a soprano might delight in.

It was this work, with its strikingly Purcellian idiom, that produced her most stylish and animated playing, but her response to the wit of Debussy's Sonata was hardly less keen, and there was much that was beautiful and moving in her intimate, introspective and amazingly mature performance of Bach's unaccompanied Suite in C minor. She avoided Beethoven, and found herself slightly out of her depth only in Brahms's E minor Sonata, in which the form of the weighty outer movements was not fully mastered, and her tone, through no fault of her excellent partner, Ernest Lush, did not always get through. The deep boom of the instrument was there, but the actual notes did not always penetrate.

Colin Mason, *The Guardian*

This country has produced very few string players of the first rank, but it may well be that last night's concert at Wigmore Hall revealed a cellist who will reach international rank. At sixteen Jacqueline du Pré plays with a technical assurance, a range of tone and a musical understanding that challenge comparison with those of all but the very finest cellists.

Her ability to carry through a phrase to its very end and the gravity and poise of her line-drawing were already remarkable in the finale of a Handel sonata. Her instinctive rubato in the trio of Brahms's E minor Sonata only emphasized the vigorous strength of her rhythms in general.

Brahms's last movement demands a greater volume of tone than she could quite muster (not that the duel with the piano is ever a very happy one).

But she brought to the Serenade of Debussy's Sonata a mock-rhetorical incisiveness and a gamut of colour from which only the composer's favourite silvery tone was perhaps absent . . .

Bach's unaccompanied C minor Suite showed her innate musical character. If the meditative movements were a trifle laboured and literal rather than freely expressive, this can hardly be held against so young a player.

We are accustomed to British artists who seem instinctively to divorce themselves from their music, but here is a young player whose technical accomplishments have not prevented her from being wholly committed to whatever she plays – and this is one of the first essentials of a great player.

Martin Cooper, *Daily Telegraph*

. . . Miss du Pré has already won important academic awards and has studied, *inter alia*, with Casals. She is, however, no mere industrious student and never once gave the impression of repeating a well absorbed lesson; on the contrary, she played with extraordinary maturity and assurance and in all her undertakings revealed pronounced interpretative individuality. In Handel's G minor Sonata, as elsewhere, she revealed an innate sense of style, produced a pure, rich tone and established a firm yet flexible line. The same virtues were again applied to the more searching test of Bach's unaccompanied Suite No. 5 in C minor; throughout, the technical control of an intractable instrument was consummate, while the clarity of articulation and luminous phrasing were *per se* a source of unstinted admiration. More important, the effect of the performance as a whole was to present unaccompanied Bach, for once, not as a dry academic exercise or essay in virtuosity, but as living music, and it is not an exaggeration to aver that such playing reminded us forcibly of Casals in his prime. Miss du Pré was fully equal to the

exacting demands of Brahms's Sonata in E minor; her reading had all
the requisite length and breadth of phrase, and to this was added a
warmth and expressive eloquence that seemed incredible in one so
young. Versatility was further demonstrated in a keenly perceptive
account of Debussy's elusive Sonata (1915) to which Miss du Pré
brought a remarkable range of tone-colour, and a long and taxing
evening ended with Maurice Maréchal's transcription of Falla's
Suite Populaire Espagnole. England has produced many capable
pianists, but only two cellists of the first order, both of whom have
now retired; if Miss du Pré continues to develop at her present pace
she should soon attain international status. She was greatly helped
by Ernest Lush who once again proved to be an ideal collaborator.

Musical Opinion

From Evelyn, Con Amore
by
LADY BARBIROLLI

Jackie was very fond of John, my husband. I believe she completely trusted his opinions and advice, which she would always listen to and follow assiduously.

She has such great vitality and warmth. John always said that all she ever needed to learn was to 'govern it a little'.

It was at one of the Suggia Awards that I heard her for the first time. John was one of the adjudicators and I had gone along to collect him. All the other adjudicators knew me and I was invited in to listen, instead of having to wait outside in the car.

Jackie, I would think, must have been about ten years old; her mother was accompanying her, but I am ashamed to say I cannot remember what she was playing. I do recall, though, being absolutely fascinated by what I heard. The girl was clearly so gifted, so immediately compelling. I still remember John talking enthusiastically about her as we drove away, and saying with absolute conviction: 'Well, today we have heard someone really special.'

I discovered later that Jackie herself had vivid recollections of that occasion. She told me that John had been most kind to her. In fact, she said he had helped her to tune her cello; being rather nervous, she had particularly appreciated this. As a cellist himself, he no doubt felt he should be helpful to a fellow instrumentalist.

Some while after John died I went to visit Jackie when she was living in Hampstead. It was soon after her illness had developed and she was in bed at the time. We had dinner together and talked about her predicament. I remember being amazed at her incredibly philosophical attitude, which was quite wonderful to witness. She told me that she considered she had enjoyed a jolly good run, even

Associated Press

*Jackie, winner of the Queen's Prize in 1960, presents the
traditional bouquet to the Queen Mother. Sir Charles
Kennedy-Scott, President of the Musicians' Benevolent Fund, is
in the centre*

though she was so young, and that this was something which was
not given to many people. She said that she was prepared to accept
the situation and make the best of things in whatever way she
could. I cannot believe that this is always so, although it was her
attitude that day. It is difficult for anyone, no matter how resilient
of spirit, to be resigned to the harsh blows of fate with constant
equanimity.

Now I would like to move back in time to 1967 and a really joyous
occasion. John had been asked to conduct the Verdi Requiem in
Israel, and our arrival there coincided with the end of the Six-Day
War.

There were some nine scheduled performances of the Requiem,
which were being given in memory of Toscanini and to mark the
twenty-fifth anniversary of the Israel Philharmonic Orchestra.
When we arrived at the airport we were met by the manager and
directors who thought the Requiem was far too solemn a work with
which to celebrate Israel's victory, and it was immediately agreed

that a change be made to Beethoven's Choral Symphony, a really appropriate choice and one which would use the soloists who were already there. I think the only rather disappointed person was Janet Baker who had particularly been looking forward to singing the Verdi.

It also transpired that Jackie and Danny had chosen the day following our arrival on which to be married in Jerusalem. They returned later to Tel Aviv for the reception and celebrations in the evening, which fortunately we were able to attend. It was a wonderful party, particularly so because we were celebrating not only the Barenboim wedding, but the fact that peace had once again returned to the troubled land of Israel.

A source of the greatest possible satisfaction to me were the television Master Classes. Maybe I was a little biased because I was so overjoyed to see Jackie making a comeback as a public performer, which by nature is basically her métier. I thought the programmes were really good; the fact of Jackie being unable to demonstrate mattered to me not in the least. The only minor comment I could possibly make is that, early in the series, she was so eager to help, advise and instruct that sometimes she would give the students hardly sufficient time to get going! I felt throughout each programme what a great inspiration she was and it was this that made them so compelling for me.

Teaching has provided a new dimension in Jackie's musical life. 'I have had to become far more articulate than I used to be,' she told me when we were comparing notes on teaching. 'When you can't demonstrate, words must be chosen with the greatest care and precision.'

There were times when I recall my husband saying that in his opinion she was touched by genius, and that was a word he never used lightly. So I was particularly happy last year, as President of the Incorporated Society of Musicians, when it was decided to give Jackie the Society's medal for outstanding musical achievements. The award was made not only for her work as a performer, but in recognition of her new and valuable contributions as a teacher.

There is a photograph of Jackie of which I am particularly fond. She sent it to me about two years ago. It was taken in the artists' room of a Moscow concert hall; on the back she has written: 'From Russia with love'. For her friendship, her remarkable contribution to music, her sense of humour and indomitable blitheness of spirit, I reciprocate sincerely: from Evelyn *con amore*.

Fiery Talent
by
GERALD MOORE

It is lèse-majesté in my opinion, concerning an artist of international repute, to want to know who was his teacher. Why must we be reminded that this past-master of his art had to be taught to draw a bow on the open string or play the C major scale on the pianoforte?

I now propose to commit the very offence which I condemn. In extenuation I must add that, like others, I have been a fortunate witness of the blossoming of Jacqueline du Pré from the precocious brilliance of her childhood to the radiant artist of authority that she is now. Therefore, with apologies, back to the drawing-board.

Under the auspices of the Arts Council of Great Britain, 'A Gift for the Cello in memory of Madame Guilhermina Suggia' was founded a year or so after the Portuguese cellist died, its object being to help promising students of the instrument. Sir John Barbirolli, who was a cellist before becoming a conductor, Lionel Tertis, Arnold Trowell and other distinguished string players and musicians were enlisted as a panel of adjudicators under the chairmanship of Eric Thompson, to hear these annual auditions.

When Jacqueline du Pré first appeared in 1955, she was ten years old, scarcely taller than her cello; her auditors were electrified after she had been playing for only half a minute. It was not until her third performance for the panel that I heard her for the first time; she was then thirteen, and it was obvious to us all that here was a genius in the making. I heard this amazing child for three successive years and her talent continued to flame. She was a bonfire.

Every musician knows when he faces the public that the first essential, before one single note is sounded, is concentration; every

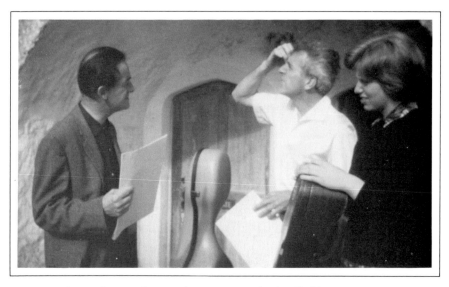

With Paul Tortelier and George Malcolm (left) at Dartington
Hall, 1961

other consideration must be banished from his mind. Only the
music matters. He attacks! He does not indulgently allow himself a
little time to 'warm up' or 'to get in voice'. Whether the player is a
seasoned professional performing to a large audience or a child
playing to a group of grey-beards on a jury, the impression made by
the very first phrase has its effect. The truth of this was made plain
at this particular audition. Before Jackie appeared, we listened to
several talented youngsters. One of them, a young cellist of some
fourteen summers, had been playing for less than a minute when a
member of the panel sitting next to me hissed in my ear, 'This boy is
asleep.' This neighbour, breathing fire, was none other than Lionel
Tertis, in his nineties and wide awake.

Then Jackie appeared and she attacked.

What a responsibility to have such a girl as this under your
musical tutelage! To this day she is grateful to William Pleeth for all
the guidance he gave her. Here is an excerpt from his letter of
recommendation when she was heard at the Suggia Award for the
first time:

> She is the most outstanding cellistic and musical talent I have met so
> far, to which she adds incredible maturity of mind. I am of the
> opinion that she will have a great career and deserves every help to
> this end.

I quote this letter, not only as a compliment to Jackie, but to pay tribute to the generosity and unselfishness of Pleeth. A teacher, once in a blue moon, suddenly finds that a young student under his care is unusually gifted and is sometimes loth to part with him or her for fear of losing the glory that will rub off on to the teacher. Years ago I wanted a young cellist to go to Casals for lessons and she was as keen as mustard, but it was a fight to induce the London teacher to part with her. 'What can Casals give her that I cannot?' she demanded of me. Similarly, I know of a gifted singer whose brilliant voice is eminently suitable for the operatic stage, but when I made the suggestion to the young hopeful that a year's course at an operatic school was essential, I was told: 'I shall never, never leave my present teacher.' This attitude is not the fault of the student but of the teacher.

One can say that William Pleeth taught Jacqueline du Pré wonderfully and then, when the time was ripe and the moment opportune, helped to launch her into less sheltered waters to broaden her outlook and enrich her mind.

By the expression 'less sheltered waters' I am not suggesting that when she went to Moscow to study with Mstislav Rostropovich he gave her a rough time! He was, as always, an inspiration to the girl and when she returned to England an international career was opening out for her.

She had developed mentally and physically, musically and technically. Beneath the quiet surface were hidden all the emotion, the feeling, the sensitivity of your finished artist. In addition, to give them expression, were a wonderful bowing arm and a string hand strong and sure; intonation impeccable – quality of tone beautiful.

I partnered Guilhermina Suggia (often alluded to as the Teresa Carreño of the violoncello) very frequently and we were great friends, but I think that Jackie's tone had more body. I do not say this to belittle the Portuguese artist, for she would herself have acknowledged it, so ungrudging was she in her appreciation of her fellow players. In fact she played like a woman, whereas the English girl had the strength of a man. (To acquire a big tone becomes a fetish with some cellists and often – like singers forcing their voices – they gain it only at the expense of quality. Hans Kindler from the Netherlands forsook his instrument to become a conductor of the Washington Symphony Orchestra, but in his playing days would pretend to identify rival cellists in this manner: When asked: 'Do you remember X?' he would answer, after affecting to cudgel his

Playing the Elgar Cello Concerto at the Royal Festival Hall, 1962

brains for a moment, 'Oh yes, now I remember him. Small tone.')

Strength, however, was probably the last thing that Jackie thought about when she played, for she was simply obsessed by the music and flung herself into it with utter lack of self-consciousness. I nearly wrote 'with fierce concentration' but the adjective would be false, for I have seen her and Daniel Barenboim at public performances exchange smiles or ecstatic glances during the course of some inspired dialogue between cello and piano.

There are no half measures with this young woman and there were no half measures when she was seized by multiple sclerosis. It was not a gradual attack which would enable her to carry on for a few years before it affected those wonderful hands and arms; it struck completely and with devastating speed. And this is where her greatness of soul has won the love of us all, for she has a radiance rising above all physical impediments.

'Wait a moment,' said Barenboim after one of his concerts, 'there is a beautiful girl coming along in a minute', and there she was in her wheelchair looking at her husband with love and pride, shedding gladness all round her.

And Danny, illustrious musician that he is, wanted everywhere the world over as a conductor, puts his beloved wife first and his dazzling career second. So as not to be too far apart from Jacqueline, he only accepts engagements that necessitate him being away from her for two or three days at the most, within an hour or so of flying time from their home in London. He and his wife are still perfect partners and no greater tribute can be paid than that.

I listened to her melodious speaking voice on the radio recently, and her high heart, her love of beauty, were made clear when she told her interlocutor that she hoped to express in poetry what she could no longer express in music. This was modesty indeed for she expresses herself cogently, kindly and to the point, in her Master Classes.

I shall always treasure the moments when I was associated with this wonderful artist; they were all too few, but I am grateful for them.

(Adapted from Farewell Recital, *London 1978)*

Gerald Moore joking with Jackie, from Country Life, *28 August 1969*

Jackie Talking to
William Wordsworth, 1969

When I married I became a convert to Judaism; it all seemed to happen quite naturally. I love Israel and the people. Marrying into a Jewish family presented no problems at all. It all seems to flow so smoothly.

I never had particular leanings towards any specific religion before I became a convert. The only feelings I had were, I suppose, of something abstract when I prayed. I think the thing that made it so easy for me is that the Jewish religion is perhaps the most abstract. Since I was a child I had always wanted to be Jewish, not in any definite way, because, of course, I didn't understand anything about it. Possibly it may somehow have been to do with the fact that so many musicians are Jewish. It seemed to be something that went with the profession and something somehow almost related to music. There's no person or image with Judaism or with music – nothing completely tangible – so the two things for me seem somehow bound together.

Life is incredibly important and every minute one must try to cherish. Since I changed my religion, I don't think I've made any startling leaps in character. This is something I have always felt I must try to nourish and improve every day.

I would like to think I play better now than before I was married. If I do, then it's most certainly due to Daniel's help and influence. To have such a common understanding and feeling about music is a wonderful basis on which to build a life together, a good 'compost heap'. To be compatible in every way and yet to offend each other musically would have been a ghastly situation leading, I suppose, to eventual disaster. Of course, don't imagine we think completely identically about everything in music. We are simply agreed about basic principles. There is plenty of latitude left for trimmings and other details. And every performer must be allowed scope for individuality. I hope I'm a help in some ways to Daniel, too. Apart from all the normal joys of marriage, it's marvellous, when one has a musical problem, to be able to nudge someone in bed and say: 'Hey, what about this or that?'

It always annoys me that I need a lot of sleep. Sometimes more than the usual eight hours. Now, Daniel doesn't. Another failing which annoys me considerably is not practising as much as possible. It's fine as long as one's in trim, but if there's stuff to learn it tends to be left to the last minute. I suppose I'm not as self-disciplined as I should be. I love being alone in a room with a cello and just playing. It's a most exhilarating feeling; the practising part, though, I'm not quite so good at.

I find it very hard to appreciate much modern music. Maybe it's sheer laziness on my part, but I find I really don't like the sounds. When related to the cello, I like them still less because I feel they're anti the instrument. It's quite hard because, being a young musician, one's supposed to know about it and to be in with it all. There are, of course, some things that I like, but not very much and I really do try. I suppose it's so lacking in appeal for me I'm not keen enough to wallow in it and find out more.

Daniel really designs the whole shape of our working lives, trying to arrange for us to work together as much as possible or at least to accompany each other to engagements, otherwise we'd be in different parts of the world most of the time. We do manage in this way to get holidays together, too. We haven't had many lately but we shall do. There seems always so much activity and so many people with whom we have to be involved that days upon days go by without us being able to sit down for a quiet talk to one another. It's all most enjoyable, although there does come a longing just to be left on our own sometimes.

When I was ten I was given a scholarship to study for seven years. That was the period when I really did some pretty concentrated practising at what was, of course, the vital time. The thing was, I more or less left school when I was eleven; this was one of the conditions of the scholarship. And here is one of the problems of the English educational system: when one is very young, there is very little provision for doing anything needing special intensive study, such as music, while still continuing one's education. I was just lucky to have a very understanding headmistress, who agreed I must somehow manage my schooling with about four lessons a week. Afterwards I had a coach brush me up. So, you see, I'm really uneducated or certainly under-educated. The whole world of my schooldays was the cello and I never wanted anything else. I do sometimes regret a little of my lost learning, but never the time I spent with the cello. The problem I had is now being solved by the new schools for young musicians – the Menuhin School and the Central Tutorial School at Morley College, where my mother teaches. Their ideas are marvellous, because they give both a thorough education and the time for students to practise, which is so vitally important. When I was young there was nothing like these schools, and for me it was a question of either/or; if you wait until schooling is finished it's about ten years too late.

Greatness and Modesty
by
ANTONY HOPKINS

I first heard the name Jacqueline du Pré after a long and frankly not
very enthralling meeting of the Council of the Royal Society of Arts,
of which august body I was then a member. A small concert had
been proposed to celebrate some occasion whose significance has
now completely escaped me.

'Might I suggest Jacqueline du Pré?' said the secretary with some
diffidence. 'She's only sixteen, I know, but she's really very good.'

'If you say so,' I replied, anxious to escape from the stuffy,
smoke-filled room in which I'd spent the last three hours. And so it
was that I first met Jackie, accompanying her in some city hall on a
somewhat formal occasion that could scarcely be classified as a
concert; it was more of a diversion to entertain a not specifically
musical audience. However, even the least musical person there
must have been aware that here indeed was a formidable talent; the
glorious tone, the intuitive phrasing, the total involvement that we
all came to associate with her playing were already there. I was
naturally thrilled as I always am by exceptional gifts in the young,
and at once longed to pass on to her any knowledge of my own that
might conceivably be of help. With her mother's enthusiastic assent
it was decided that Jackie should come to me for an occasional
lesson in the appreciation of musical structure, a general widening
of her comprehension which, at that time, was instinctive rather
than intellectual.

A few days later she arrived at my home in Brook Green, a shy,
reticent schoolgirl who, in conversation, utterly belied the ex-
trovert musical personality she had displayed when her cello spoke

Erich Auerbach

Jackie, aged seventeen, in a solo appearance on television,
accompanied by her mother

for her. We spent a couple of hours talking about Form, a subject on which her ideas were surprisingly hazy; but though there were prodigious gaps in her theoretical knowledge, her musical instinct was so sure that she could absorb with ease any ideas I put to her. She was able to identify so totally with the music that I soon realized that she could bypass most of the processes by which lesser mortals arrive at their conclusions. To my sorrow the 'lessons' were soon discontinued; here was a flower that could blossom gloriously without any aid from me.

Occasionally she would come of an evening and we would play sonatas together, although her technical command was so absolute that I always felt fumble-fingered by comparison. A trio concert with Hugh Maguire in Northampton stands out as a particularly joyous occasion. It was a rare pleasure for me to find myself playing in such company, though at times Hugh and I both had to offer a gentle rebuke, pointing out that the cello wasn't supposed to lead *all* the time. If I contributed something, however small, to her musical development, it would give me a feeling of pride, for without doubt she proved to be not just a great cellist but a truly marvellous interpreter.

On one occasion, early in her career she came to Norwich to play the Schumann Concerto with me and the wholly amateur Norwich Philharmonic Orchestra. Having played the concerto with deeply poetic insight, earning an ovation from a packed hall, she enchanted us all by sitting at the back desk of the cellos for the final item, Borodin's Polovtsian Dances. It was as though an electric charge had irradiated the entire cello section and they played as never before. It was the first (and only) time that I have known a cello section to have been led from behind to such effect. I am sure that not one of the players present will forget that gesture on her part. She, the acknowledged soloist, joined with them for the sheer fun of the music, showing that she combined greatness with modesty.

The cruel extinction of her meteoric career was something to destroy one's belief in any justice, divine or otherwise. At least, though, she knows what it is to achieve an absolute summit as an artist, and in doing so to inspire not just admiration and wonder but also love.

A sketch of Jackie by Zsuzsi Roboz

A Tale of Two Cellos

When, at the age of five, Jacqueline du Pré was taken to the London Cello School to start regular lessons, she insisted, not entirely unreasonably, on taking her cello with her. It was a full-size instrument and rather larger than its youthful owner. To her great dismay it was immediately put aside by her teacher and a smaller one provided for her use. This was regarded by the young player not only with grave disappointment but also as a serious affront to her dignity.

As if by way of making amends, some ten years later, just before she was to make her professional debut at the Wigmore Hall, she received from an anonymous donor the gift of a cello made in 1672 by the master maker of stringed instruments, Antonio Stradivari.

Another five years passed by and a telephone call came from Charles Beare, the well-known London dealer in stringed instruments. He said that he had a cello in his shop waiting for Jacqueline du Pré to try and, if she liked it, it would be given to her. It proved to be not only a glorious sounding instrument but a beautiful looking one as well. She was utterly overjoyed and immediately accepted the generous gift most gratefully.

The mysterious donor, if it was the same one as before, had been yet more lavish with the second gift. This cello was the 'Davidoff' Stradivarius, so called because it once belonged to the Russian cellist Karl Davidoff (1838–89). It was made in 1712 and the story goes that in the early nineteenth century a Count Apraxin sold the instrument to a Count Wielhorsky. The price was a Guarneri cello, a pedigree horse and about £4,000 in cash. Count Wielhorsky, to

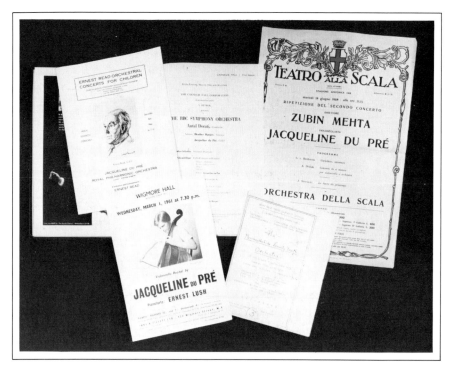

A selection of programmes and posters

celebrate his eightieth birthday in 1847, presented the cello to the young Russian virtuoso Davidoff, who kept it until he died.

Another well-known firm of London stringed instrument dealers, Alfred Hill & Sons, have recorded that the 'Davidoff' went to Paris in 1900, when it was sold to a wealthy amateur. In 1928 it again changed hands, this time going to America, where it was bought by Herbert N. Straus, a music-loving department store executive. He acquired it to complete a quartet of Stradivari instruments which were used for playing chamber music in his home.

When Mr Straus died, his widow asked Rembert Wurlitzer, then a leading firm of fine stringed instrument dealers in New York, if they would find a buyer of the 'Davidoff' for her.

When Charles Beare received a call from a London firm of solicitors asking if he would look out for a really outstanding cello to be purchased by one of their clients as a gift to Jacqueline du Pré, he immediately contacted New York and Mrs Wurlitzer brought the instrument to London where the sale was concluded. The dollar price paid was believed to have been close to six figures.

The 'Davidoff' is to the pattern of some twenty surviving Stradivari cellos which are recognized as being the very greatest of stringed instruments. Amongst these it is generally considered to rank as one of the three finest cellos in the world.

W.W.

An Angel of Warmth

by

RAYMOND ERICSON

New York Times, Saturday, 15 May 1965

Someone knows Jacqueline du Pré's worth. The twenty-year-old English cellist, who made her New York début last night in Carnegie Hall as soloist with the BBC Symphony Orchestra, was given the 'Davidoff' Stradivarius cello last year after it had been bought anonymously for an estimated $90,000, said to be the highest price paid for a stringed instrument.

Miss du Pré did not play the 'Davidoff', but used another Stradivarius, dating from 1672, also presented to her anonymously. She showed that she deserved the best.

A tall, slim blonde, Miss du Pré looked like a cross between Lewis Carroll's Alice and one of those angelic instrumentalists in Renaissance paintings. And, in truth, she played like an angel, one with extraordinary warmth and sensitivity.

Her vehicle was Elgar's Cello Concerto. It dates from 1919, which made it eligible for the orchestra's series of six programmes here, devoted to twentieth-century works. But it is pure romanticism in style and flavour and could just as easily have been composed in the nineteenth century.

Miss du Pré and the concerto seemed made for each other, because her playing was so completely imbued with the romantic spirit. Her tone was sizeable and beautifully burnished. Her technique was virtually flawless, whether she was playing the sweeping chords that open the concerto, sustaining a ravishing pianissimo tone, or keeping the fast repeated-note figures in the scherzo going at an even pace.

Astonishing was the colour she brought to the concerto's

dominant lyricism, the constant play of light and delicacy of emotion in a fresh, spontaneous, yet perfectly poised way.

At the end of the concert Miss du Pré was brought back to the stage again and again by the large audience, and she was applauded by her fellow musicians in the orchestra. One performance does not indicate the range of an artist, but at least in the Elgar concerto the cellist was superb.

Sharing a Language
by
YEHUDI MENUHIN

How rare it is and what a joy to write with full, free heart and mind about someone one really loves, respects and admires.

Not, I hope, that I have often been a Happy Hypocrite singing praises slightly off-key in an effort to fulfil a courtesy out of duty and demand. For I have been singularly fortunate in my friends and colleagues, and can it be that musicians really are of such a high standard as nice human beings? That question has to remain rhetorical out of modesty, for I am one of the band myself and would dread to think I were perhaps the exception to the rule I have just presented above.

But to return to the young friend and colleague about whom I am writing these words: Jacqueline du Pré. Jackie has always held a very special place in my heart from the time when, as a member of a jury of three, I first heard her play at the Royal College, for seldom can one say that one has been suddenly inspired, not by a professional of long standing and experience, but by a sixteen-year-old girl whose whole language was music, who had that marvellous conviction and comprehension of what she was saying that can only spring from having been born trailing clouds of glory. It is not necessary to talk about technique, for it was her complete control of the cello that freed her to play as she did, to sing the phrases with that full-blooded and yet so sensitive approach that makes her unique and that is her great gift.

To this day I can recall the elation she brought me and all the other listeners whom she set alight with the excitement of her own joy and intoxication with the music. I remember whispering to one

FROM SIR MALCOLM SARGENT, 9 ALBERT HALL MANSIONS, LONDON, S.W. 7.

30th November 1964.

Dear Jacqueline

Alas I have not had a chance of meeting
you with regard to the Delius Cello Concerto -
I have been abroad and am just off again, but
I shall be here from the 13th December and
shall telephone you hoping that we can perhaps
meet and can have an hour together looking at
the Concerto, preparing for the recording.

I am very anxious that we should do a
public performance of this, and the Royal Choral
Society have agreed to make half of one of
their concerts Delius and with you as the
soloist.   It is of course a choral concert, but
we shall have this as a solo item with the Delius
Concerto.   The date is March 22nd 1966.   Would
you please keep this date for me and let me
know when this is definitely booked.   We can
then set to work with your Agents if necessary
but I wanted you to be prepared for this as I do
hope you can come.

all good wishes -

Yours very sincerely,

Malcolm Sargent

Miss Jacqueline du Pre,
63 Portland Place, W.1.

*Sir Malcolm Sargent's letter and Jackie with Sir Malcolm and
Ronald Kinloch-Anderson during a break in the recording of the
Delius Cello Concerto, 1965*

of my neighbours, 'I'm sure she is studying with William Pleeth' – and indeed she was.

Shortly afterwards, as President of the National Trust Society's concerts, I asked her whether she would care to join my sister, Hephzibah, and myself in giving a trio recital at Osterley Park. It was quite a new sensation for both of us, I think, suddenly to realize that we no longer represented the younger musicians as we had for so long, but were now sedately in our early forties and that this passionate and gifted young sprig probably felt, exactly as we had, that mixture of adventure and the unknown adding itself to the sheer joy of playing. If I turn aside here to say that we still feel the same thrill, I hope it will be understood as an example of the good fortune of the musician to be so constantly renewed and not that dear Jackie had to join a pair of deep-frozen prodigies. Be that as it may, we had a lovely time together, the rehearsals were minimal for we found we shared the same language. What more can one say about a sixteen-year-old girl barely out of the Royal College who was at one and the same time sweet and easy in character, totally unselfconscious, and yet sure, steady and utterly musical?

She brought the same combination of ease and profundity, too, when she joined Louis Kentner and myself in what I believe was her first BBC broadcast not long after this. And there were other joys: when Jackie and Maurice Gendron joined in the slow movement of the Schubert two-cello Quintet for a BBC programme called *The Menuhins at Home*, or again when were were all together with Alberto Lysy's Camerata at Sermoneta and we shared that same natural, joyous music-making that is the dream of all musicians. It was there, incidentally, that she first confided in me about a worrying sensation in her right arm – the first indication, I suppose, of the impending nightmare that would have destroyed any other young woman than Jackie. Those very qualities: strength and joy, passion and directness that were her musical voice are palpably her true character and she has proven this ineluctable fact in the wonderful way she has accepted the cruel blow that was to cut short a brilliant career.

But has it cut it short? To my way of thinking, only in the sad fact that she can no longer perform, but not in any other way, for she is transmuting her tragedy into what is virtually a triumph – a triumph of mind over matter, making of herself a shining example to all other sufferers from her disease. What she is in fact doing is actively analysing that word 'dis-ease', rejecting the first syllable and only accepting the second, easing herself from her plight in those inspiring Master Classes, showing with a lightness and intensity that nothing is ever lost. Here is Jacqueline du Pré, the deep musical mind, the intuitive musician offering all her gifts and her experience with generosity, skill and gladness. Here is the living creature of whom Shakespeare wrote:

> In sweet music is such art
> Killing care and grief of heart . . .

And by her side all this time she has had Danny, whose character, like hers, is a reflection of his music: highly gifted, sensitive, sincere, strong and patient – a wonderful piece of good fortune for her and a man for whom I feel the deepest respect.

Looking at her, listening to her, one feels humble before such a spirit, ashamed of ever indulging in self-pity, proud to have shared, however little, in music-making with her.

Bless you, Jackie, you are a lesson to us all.

A change of instrument: Jackie on the violin, Yehudi Menuhin on the cello, Ernst Wallfisch in the centre

Jackie by Zsuzsi Roboz

'The Bolt of Cupid'
by
DAME JANET BAKER

Daniel Barenboim and I used to give recitals together and he was a wonderful pianist with whom to work. It was not until much later in our association that I met Jackie.

In 1967 I went out to Israel where I was to sing in nine performances of the Verdi Requiem, conducted by Sir John Barbirolli. We arrived just after the Six-Day War and, not unreasonably, we were asked to change the programme. Everywhere, as was to be expected, there was a generally infectious air of celebration and rejoicing. From a purely professional point of view I must confess I was most disappointed; I had been looking forward with great anticipation to singing Verdi with Sir John. It is, after all, a much more satisfying undertaking for singers than Beethoven's Ninth Symphony which took its place.

A great compensation for my disappointment was being in Israel then, a time when, quite unexpectedly, at least for me, Daniel and Jackie decided to arrange their own victory celebrations by getting married. I was fortunate in being able to join in the festivities and go to the wedding reception in Tel Aviv. Jackie's parents had flown out specially from England and, I seem to remember, were staying with the visiting musicians and singers at the Orchestra House.

It was all most exciting; the whole time was quite extraordinary. We were all very conscious of participating in what would be regarded as a historic event. In addition to this there was the wonderful personal aspect of the wedding, with the joy and happiness which these two young people were able to share with their families and friends. The two events, one momentous, the other intimate, somehow seemed to complement each other emotionally.

It was an unbelievable time to have chosen for a wedding, the very atmosphere seemed charged with wonder and rejoicing. Every-where feelings ran high; Jerusalem was again a united City and the Wailing Wall of Solomon's Temple had been uncovered. Relief and happiness abounded; it seemed to be cascading through the ancient narrow streets and in the midst of it all was this radiant couple. Their sheer blissful elation was really something to have seen; it was such as to have left the deepest of impressions. Far removed from the proverbial happy pair, they were somehow touched, it seemed to me, by an ethereal magic. I remember thinking then that I could well have echoed Oberon: 'Yet mark'd I where the bolt of Cupid fell'.

In the ensuing years, every time we saw them in New York or London, at concerts or around a supper table, the intensity of feeling between them was so clearly apparent. I can so distinctly recall thinking that the affinity between them was so extraordinarily vital as to seem, in human terms, impossible to maintain. They were rather like two shooting stars and every time I saw them I expected to find them orbiting more slowly, calming down as couples do in most marriages. Sometimes, as I watched them, I would have the direst fears that so all-consuming a relationship would burn itself out.

In retrospect, of course, one sees what the cruel fates decreed; how a distillation of an emotional lifetime was crowded into just a few years. With hindsight one is so deeply grateful that they had this quite remarkable time together. The energy emitted by the two of them was quite staggeringly overpowering. They were so closely involved with each other on so many levels, it was a prospect of really great beauty, with mutual involvement enough for seven lifetimes.

Another remarkable relationship which particularly impresses me is that between Daniel and Zubin Mehta. I cannot ever remember seeing a closer comradeship between two men, with such a genuine concern and understanding for each other's personal as well as professional problems. It is clearly a very rare friendship indeed.

Unlike so many of us, Jackie has always had the knack of 'switching off' when she has finished work and this is really a tremendous asset, resulting in her being such an extremely well balanced person. There was an occasion after a concert when we were together in a small supper party which included Pinky and Genie Zukerman; across the table relaxed fun and witty exchanges were being enjoyed between Jackie and Genie. Then, without warning, to the considerable surprise of other diners, these two young, beautiful women resorted to pelting each other with paper pellets. The rest of us were just busy talking about our work as, I fear, we are rather too frequently prone to do. But Jackie has such a natural ability to digress into frolicsome forms of relaxation which is a joy to see and the envy of those of us who are more inhibited. I have seen this tendency in many great musicians: a great sense of enjoyment of nonsense and trivia, as important in its way as the work on a concert platform.

Always a deeply committed musician, Jackie has a facet of her character which sometimes seems to be that of a disarmingly natural child, added to which she has a highly developed sense of the ridiculous. Fortunately, even now, in spite of everything, she still retains that sense of humour and unreality.

Cardus Pays Homage

With the arrival in Edinburgh of multitudes of Londoners and other aliens, the Scottish summer collapsed last night, and, in spite of torrents of rain, the Usher Hall was packed to hear the London Symphony Orchestra play the fifth symphony of Schubert, Dvořák's Cello Concerto, with Jacqueline du Pré as the soloist, and Bartok's Concerto for Orchestra, all conducted by Istvan Kertesz...

After the elaborate orchestral introduction of the Dvořák Cello Concerto, Jacqueline du Pré attacked her instrument with so much energy and thrash of bow that I said to myself 'she is going to break a string', which she did, soon after her first entrance, following the glorious horn melody. She apologized to the audience amid universal applause, retired from our sight for repairs and another string. Her reappearance was the occasion for another ovation from an audience whose reactions had been changed from the musical and aesthetic to the sporting. The concerto was not resumed from the beginning, but from the most convenient bridge passage. The young cellist was not at all put out of mood; and in fact she played with a range and controlled musical energy surpassing even the best I had heard before of her rare and richly endowed art. Her soft playing and her variations of tone in the slow movement were simply beautiful. Not since Casals have I heard a cello sing with so much lyrical warmth as Jacqueline strokes or caresses from it. And added to heart-easing song was strength and breadth of attack and phrase. This Jacqueline du Pré is nature's most precious gift to English music since the advent of Kathleen Ferrier. Pianists are two a penny nowadays; cellists are as scarce as sunshine in the England of the summer of 1968. And a superb executant of music, an artist of her or his instrument, is a more valuable asset to our music than any second-rate and supposedly 'creative' composer . . .

Neville Cardus, *The Guardian*, 26 August 1968

Casals Is Deeply Moved

Earlier this week, a younger musician brought tears to Casals's eyes with a performance of the Elgar Cello Concerto, a work he had performed in London in the early 1920s before King George V.

Here it was Jacqueline du Pré, the twenty-three-year-old English cellist, who performed the difficult piece, with Daniel Barenboim, her twenty-six-year-old Israeli husband, conducting the orchestra.

Miss du Pré, a tall girl with long wavy fair hair, was called back to the stage six times by a standing ovation. Backstage, after the concert, the two young artists were embraced by Casals, who had listened to the performance from a high-backed chair placed in the wings.

'I always said you can't be English with such a temperament,' he told the beaming Miss du Pré. 'Of course it must come from your father's French ancestors. It was beautiful, beautiful. Every note in its place and every emphasis so right. Beautiful.'

Henry Raymont, *New York Times*, 8 June 1969

Musicality Comes First
by
PLACIDO DOMINGO

I have heard Jackie in performance only twice. In 1969 I was singing in *Carmen* in Tel Aviv and I heard that a concert was to be given in Caesarea, which Daniel Barenboim was conducting. Naturally I knew of Jacqueline's great reputation, but I was certainly not prepared for the incredible brilliance of her artistry. Her striking appearance, the flowing blonde hair, sitting there with her cello waiting for her moment of entry, with all the compelling appeal of a modern Mélisande. From the moment she began to play I found myself hypnotized by her. Immediately I was aware of the artistry, concentration and power that was being marshalled to make her cello sing in a way I had never heard a cello sound before. Those were my first impressions and it was indeed a memorable experience. After the concert I met Jackie and Daniel and we have become the greatest of friends; although, owing to our various engagements, it has never been possible to see as much of them as I would wish.

The second time that the three of us met they were playing the famous Piano Quintet in A major by Schubert, with Zubin Mehta, Pinchas Zukerman and Itzhak Perlman, of which Christopher Nupen made a splendid film which has been seen on television all over the world. This blithe and lyrical quintet earned its nickname from the fact that the fourth movement is a set of variations on the tune of Schubert's song 'Die Forelle' – The Trout. This was another great occasion for me. I was able to attend the rehearsals as well as the actual performance when it was filmed. Again I recognized Jackie's amazing qualities and marvelled at this superb way of making music. Such a remarkable band of talent combining together, not only to produce a memorable performance for an audience, but the better to enjoy their own music-making. Mingled with my feelings of appreciation and enjoyment, I remember experiencing a great sense of regret that I could not be up there on the platform taking part and enjoying it with them. I am not an envious person, but I never before felt so strongly that I did not want to be just sitting there as a member of the audience. I had a tremendous desire to be up there with them, singing some libretto for tenor which, alas, of course, does not exist.

Sometimes when I had been recording with Daniel I would go home with him to see Jackie. On one such occasion I happened to mention to her that my favourite musical instrument is the cello, which I always like to imitate with my voice, especially in the legato passages. So, as soon as I had said this, Jacqueline decided she was going to start teaching me to play the cello. There is not yet much I can play. Not being very often in London with much spare time I have so far only had about a couple of lessons; consequently I am not yet a virtuoso, although I am really amazed at what Jackie has managed to teach me in such a very short time. When she came to a performance of *Otello* at Covent Garden, I mentioned to her that when I am next in London I will bring my younger son, who is now a teenager – he is also named Placido – and he is studying the cello and I much hope that she will teach him. He is doing very well with his studies and maybe it would be an opportunity for me to continue my so-called lessons. You see, previously I was a very bad pupil because I found it so difficult to separate the feeling of playing an instrument like the piano from the entirely different technique of wrist and arm movements needed for bowing which Jackie tried to explain to me. I found this extremely difficult. Anyway, I was awfully pleased to be told that, in spite of my problems, I made 'a good sound'. From her that was a great compliment.

The incredible thing to me is how seldom in life people will accept sickness in the way she does. She is so wonderfully philosophical. I feel that her love of human beings and music are so very vital and sustaining for her. Her Master Classes are quite wonderful. I do believe that music is for her a really great companion and motivating force. I have to confess that I could not honestly say that, in similar circumstances, I could rely on myself to react so magnificently.

I am very thrilled that on various occasions she has come to the

opera. She came to see *La Fanciulla del West, Luisa Miller* and *L'Africaine*, besides *Otello*. This indicates to me that she gets great enjoyment from opera, otherwise I am quite sure she would not come. I had reason to notice how intently Jackie listens to opera from remarks she made about a recording Daniel and I were making of *La Damnation de Faust*. I was singing an A flat when Daniel stopped and asked me to do it piano – really in head-voice. Her comment later was that it was so interesting to hear it done both ways and being able to make comparison. She went on to say she preferred the A flat to be soft because it was more in context, having a far greater feeling of musicality than doing it mezzo forte. She said she could never make herself accept anything that sacrificed musicality to theatricality.

Whenever I come to London I always look forward to getting together with Jackie because I really enjoy her company and sharing her love of music. In fact I think of it as an injection because I find that just by talking with her she can give me a renewed love of life in all its many aspects. My great regret is that I am not able to spend more time with her or even to make music with her. My piano playing is only very average, but one day I would so love to accompany her when she is playing the cello. I shall live in hope.

The Importance of
Being a Teacher

by

SIR ROBERT MAYER

I am not absolutely certain, but I can only think that I must have first heard about Jacqueline du Pré from William Pleeth. Of course I have always known him to be not only an excellent teacher of the cello but a very lively person and, what is most annoying, insufficiently recognized. It has always been a great source of surprise to me that people should want to rush off to so-called celebrated teachers abroad when we have such outstanding ones in this country. To me it is all nonsense.

The Attlee government did an unprecedented thing in Britain by agreeing to support the arts through the Council for the Encouragement of Music and the Arts (CEMA), now known as the Arts Council of Great Britain. We teach children important dates at school and we should most surely teach them that date, which was 1945. Like Pandora's Box, this released great artistic forces which we never knew existed. We were to discover that there were so many artists destined to become internationally famous because of this revolutionary move to help the arts. Perhaps this may seem a far cry from my subject, but it is not. I think we have to thank the enlightened Attlee government for Jacqueline du Pré and many other brilliant artists who have emerged as a result of the encouragement offered by public subsidy for orchestras, theatres and artists.

Jackie was not much older than sixteen when she first played for our children's concerts. She and I have met together many times; after all, the musical fraternity is a fairly small circle. There is something I remember particularly. It was some years ago and I think perhaps it was at the Austrian Institute and I expect there must have been some distinguished Austrian musicians playing. I distinctly recall seeing Jackie somewhere at the back of the room near the door, watching very intently. I think, although I cannot be absolutely certain, that she was watching Danny Barenboim who was at the piano. She appeared to be absolutely galvanized. I should be surprised if I am wrong because such a recollection cannot be invented. Of course, I must have met her between the children's concerts and that time at the Austrian Institute, not necessarily with William Pleeth but with someone or other. And then, very soon, she became that extraordinary player who was eventually to marry Barenboim. I like to think my strong recollection of her watching him playing was in some strange way prophetic.

I meet her now mainly in concert halls. When she goes everyone knows she is there. I hear, too, a lot about her teaching and her highly successful Master Classes. When I met her recently I told her that next time she was invited out to dinner by one of our many mutual friends, perhaps she could arrange for me to have an invitation for the same day, since we both frequently enjoyed our friends' hospitality but always on separate occasions. Because of her illness and the fact that I am immobilized by arthritis (to say nothing of being more than a century on this earth), we both rely for mobility on wheelchairs. So, when Greek meets Greek I think maybe we should have dinner together.

Today we live in an age of materialism and real values are distorted. It all seems to be a matter of how much you have got in the bank. So, I am particularly pleased and interested that Jackie is giving lessons. This is something of great importance and not mere materialistic value. It is perhaps a cliché now to say London is the musical centre of the world but it is nevertheless a fact. It has more opera houses and orchestras than anywhere else. Only one thing is missing: no one comes to London specifically to learn musician-ship. Not, that is, in the way that in my young days they went to teachers abroad. Then they would go to Frankfurt for piano, Leipzig for conducting, Dresden for singing and to Dr Boulanger in Paris for general musicality. I believe there is now a great opportunity to make London the seat of musical learning.

The first step is for the professors at our musical colleges to be properly paid instead of getting the pittance they now receive. Even though they were recently given what was thought to be a large increase, they are still miserably underpaid. The great teachers, like

Time Inc.

A joke with Mstislav Rostropovich

Eva Turner, for instance, who now teaches privately, and Alfred Brendel, who both plays and teaches, are here in London, although for some of them it means a considerable sacrifice because of taxation. In my opinion we cannot progress much further in London with musical performance, although we can go a hell of a lot further as a centre for teaching. It is most unfortunate that Jackie is now only teaching and not playing. However, one could not wish for a better or more dedicated instructor; it is something for which she most clearly has a gift.

It is really a very great pleasure for me to be able to pay tribute to Jackie and through her to draw attention to London as a prospectively great musical teaching centre. I hope there are those around who will start to recognize this and not just continue to think of London as the place for having their suits made in Savile Row.

I would like to end by mentioning that Jackie is fortunate in having a most marvellous husband. Daniel works so hard, but makes certain he is able to spend time regularly with her, even if it means that he has to cancel engagements. They both have my sincerest and warmest regards.

Fun and Laughter
by
ZUBIN MEHTA

It was in the summer of 1966, at Spoleto, in Umbria, central Italy, that I first met Jacqueline du Pré. I was doing an oratorio at the festival organized annually by Gian-Carlo Menotti; she was playing chamber music. Although I had heard of this new talent in England, so far as I can remember, I did not, on this occasion, hear her play. Early the following year we met again, this time in London at a rehearsal of the Mozart Requiem, which Daniel Barenboim was conducting with the Philharmonia Orchestra. It was in fact a chorus rehearsal and Jackie was just sitting there listening. This occurred to me at the time as being rather odd and I recall it set me wondering and possibly doing a little speculating.

I had then heard not a word of anything that was most probably afoot. No doubt others of their friends may well have been better informed. My friendship with Daniel is of necessity mainly conducted by long distance telephone, which does not give the opportunities to say and discuss all one would wish; person to person meetings are regrettably few.

Later in 1967 we were all involved in going to Israel. This was to prove a momentous time for the three of us. Jackie and Daniel had arrived eight days before me to give recitals at the Kibbutzim; with Israel at war they felt they must make what contribution they could. It seemed extremely doubtful if the concerts I was scheduled to conduct would ever take place, nevertheless I was determined somehow to get to Israel. Having reached Rome, it was with the help of the Israeli ambassador there that I was allowed to board an El Al plane. It was a highly secret arrangement because the plane was carrying not passengers but arms and ammunition. The plane touched down at night, with Tel Aviv in total blackout. I was met by Zvi Haftel, head of the Israel Philharmonic Orchestra committee, who welcomed me in his pyjamas. From him I first learned that Daniel and Jackie were planning imminent matrimony. At the Orchestra House, where visiting musicians stay, I found Jackie, Daniel and his parents and Sergiu Comissiona, the Rumanian-born former conductor of the Haifa Symphony Orchestra and his wife. All were sleeping in the basement of the building, treating it as an air-raid shelter. Considering that the Israelis, in their first attack, had disposed of the Egyptian airforce, this seemed a rather excessive precaution. We all stayed awake laughing and playing jokes and virtually had no sleep at all. Poor Comissiona was the chief butt of our fun. When he went to get a glass of water, I jumped into bed with his wife. The room was in darkness when he returned and the poor fellow was extremely perplexed. Affected by the tensions of a country at war, we played these childish pranks to retain some sense of normality.

Full of confidence that the war would be over soon, we set to planning a 'victory concert'. I was to conduct, Daniel would play the Beethoven Emperor and Jackie the Schumann Cello Concerto, with the Beethoven Fifth for a big triumphant finish. Surely enough, on the following Saturday, the Gala Victory Concert took place in Jerusalem, at last a reunified city under the control of Israel. With at least half the audience in khaki, it was understandably an overwhelmingly emotional occasion, although I would concede it was not the greatest music the Israel Philharmonic had ever produced.

In the midst of the confusion of the aftermath of war, Jackie and Daniel announced that they would be married on the following Wednesday. I learned that Jackie had been having religious instruction in London, preparatory to her conversion to Judaism and that the wedding was to be strictly in the Orthodox faith, including the ritual *mikvah*, or purifying bath for the bride.

Being the only member of the wedding with transport, I had to drive the chief participants about in my borrowed car. I was absolutely determined to take part in the ceremony too, although Daniel said the rabbis would not allow me to be a witness and probably would not even ride in my car if they knew I was not a Jew.

So Daniel decided upon a plan. He told the rabbi who was to perform the ceremony that I was a recently immigrated Persian Jew

*Daniel Barenboim and Jacqueline du Pré marry in Jerusalem
immediately after the Six-Day War of June 1967*

named Moshe Cohen. In those days I knew not a word of Hebrew, but most Persian Jews did not speak the ancient language either.

Having collected a venerable rabbi, we drove him and Jackie to the *mikvah*. As we sat quietly in the waiting-room, Daniel most unexpectedly became extremely excited and began shouting at some other rabbis who were gathered in the passageway outside the waiting-room. He had good reason to be incensed, for he had realized that what was concentrating their attention was that they were peeping into the room where Jackie was standing completely naked.

Order having been restored, we all got back in the car and I drove out to what is now the Jerusalem Music Centre. It was just on the border of what then was the 'no man's land' that used to divide the City. In a small house, just below the big windmill, Daniel and Jackie were married, and at the ceremony a certain 'Moshe Cohen' held one of the poles of the *chupah*, the canopy under which the bridal couple stand.

A celebration lunch took place afterwards at the King David

Hotel. At the adjoining table, discussing Israel's future, sat David Ben-Gurion, Teddy Kollek, Mayor of Jerusalem, and Defence Minister Moshe Dayan. Discussion at the wedding table was about organizing a hastily arranged goodwill tour of the United States and Canada by the Israel Philharmonic Orchestra. It was to be a fund-raising effort to help replenish the depleted national coffers. The plan was for Jackie, Daniel and myself to start the tour by repeating the Victory Concert in New York. It was hoped we would then be able to find others who would volunteer their services. David Ben-Gurion attended the wedding reception that evening, and Sir John and Lady Barbirolli, Dame Janet Baker and other visiting musicians and singers were taken there in force to offer their good wishes to the newly-weds. A while later Daniel, Jackie and I flew off together for New York to launch the benefit tour of the orchestra.

When the three of us are together fun, jokes and usually some pranks are sure to be included in the schedule. Such an occasion was the filming of the 'Trout' Quintet. It was just one big joke; nobody took it seriously and it has become a classic. I must immediately qualify that statement by adding that it was all fun and laughter until we began to play the music; there is no joking with music, let there be absolutely no misunderstanding about that.

At that time, in 1969, I had been married to my wife, Nancy, for only a month and I was most concerned at the prospect of leaving her to go to London for the Schubert Quintet concert and film, as well as having to make a recording of *Il Trovatore* while I was there.

Daniel was musical director of the South Bank Music Festival in those days and one of the concerts he had arranged consisted of the 'Trout' Quintet in the first half, with *Pierrot Lunaire* by Schoenberg after the interval. The filming took place prior to the concert and when it came to the final rehearsal in the Queen Elizabeth Hall, we all agreed at one point to switch instruments, just for laughs and to see if we could raise any comments from Christopher Nupen and his film crew. I went to the piano and I showed Daniel how to manage a few notes on my string bass. Itzhak Perlman took the cello, which, in fact, he can play a little. Pinky Zukerman, who was playing viola, took over the violin and Jackie tried to play a little on the viola.

We were all falling about laughing mainly because nobody seemed to have noticed what we were doing, so intent was the concentration on lining up the camera shots and listening to the instructions of director Chris Nupen. Well, maybe our antics were noticed and there was tacit agreement to let us carry on with our little game. In any case it could not be continued for long because none of us could manage much more than about sixteen bars on our borrowed instruments. The whole thing was not only a lot of fun but also greatly exhilarating. Basically, in simple terms, we were just five friends getting together to make music. If only it were possible to expand that notion into orchestral proportions, what a wonderful idea that would be.

Daniel and I have always been the closest of friends and Jackie has become almost like a sister to me, our lives have always intermingled. It is the greatest loss in all our lives that this girl, not simply a great cellist, but unique in the world of music, should not still be performing. I saw the film Christopher Nupen made about her for the first time the other day, and I have to admit that I sat there with tears in my eyes; I just could not believe how much we are missing. We have nobody comparable with her; she was like a lovely wild mustang. As soon as she took up the instrument, she had this incredible control that few instrumentalists in the history of string playing have ever possessed.

Having played the Dvořák Concerto with Jackie all over the world, I know from experience that sometimes, in the middle of a performance, she decides to play a phrase with a different fingering or maybe change a phrase itself, and she will do it without even the slightest qualms. Now, few instrumentalists would dare to sit in front of the Berlin Philharmonic, at a Salzburg Festival concert, and suddenly introduce a little divergence of interpretation. Many are the soloists who work eight hours a day to perfect the playing of a concerto correctly in one particular way. But Jackie possessed this flair, control, and imagination, plus a great magnetism for the audience. When she is a member of the audience at a concert I am conducting, in every bar I am conscious of her presence.

The last concert that Jackie gave in London I conducted for her. It was with the Philharmonia Orchestra in 1973; she played the Elgar Concerto and played it impeccably. After that she went to join Daniel in America and it was then that she suddenly started to cancel engagements. Nobody had the slightest idea why. She cancelled a pension fund concert with Bernstein and Zukerman, at which she was to play the Brahms Double and I think she cancelled some of her concerts in America with Daniel.

In the summer of '73 Daniel had undertaken the musical

The wedding reception. Zubin Mehta is on Jackie's left.
Aida Barenboim and Dr Enrique Barenboim, Daniel's parents,
are next to Mehta

directorship of the Israel Festival. It was planned to perform the
'Trout' again with the original five. Jackie came out to Israel, but we
played the quintet without her. She was in the audience; she just did
not want to play.

That October Israel was again at war – the Yom Kippur war. I was
there at this time and Daniel at once cancelled his engagements in
Europe and came out to join me in concerts for the Israeli forces.
Every day he telephoned Jackie. One day, when he called their
home, which was then in Hampstead, he was told she had gone to
hospital for a check-up. He asked what was wrong. The answer he
received, from an obviously uncomprehending housekeeper, was
that the doctor suspected multiple sclerosis – just like that.

At that time, like the Barenboims' housekeeper, neither Daniel
nor I had the least idea what the doctor's suspicions implied. Ten
years ago little was known about MS, except to the medical
profession, unless, of course, it came within one's own range of
experience.

Because of our ignorance of this wretched illness, when Daniel and I received the news in Israel we did not react to the enormity of what we had been told on the telephone. But, of course, we had to find out as soon as possible, so I telephoned to a doctor friend of mine to ask for an explanation. As there was only one telephone in the room, Danny came close to the instrument so that he could hear what the doctor said. That was how first he learned of the tragedy which was to come into his life. We packed him off to England just as quickly as we could, and this is not the easiest thing to do with an Israeli citizen in wartime.

This terrible sadness has drastically changed two brilliantly talented young lives. Danny has been unbelievably marvellous in his understanding. Jackie, as I told her only the other day, never complains and is always smiling, even though the illness has been going on since 1973. Whenever I ask how she is I get the same reply: 'Oh, I'm fine.' Only very occasionally does she mention suffering a little pain, although she refers to it in such a way as to lead one to believe it can easily be cured with an aspirin. They are two extraordinary human beings enduring this incredible trial. What can friends do? They feel so impotent, so helpless. They can only offer their love and support.

To this day Daniel has never accompanied another cellist, either as conductor or pianist. Frankly, I doubt if he could. As for me, on two occasions I have tried to conduct the Elgar Concerto with other cellists and I have found it impossible. It is music Jackie made so much her own. The recording of it she made with Danny in Philadelphia is, for me, the definitive performance, and one which I find I cannot listen to too often.

A Genius on Record

by

SUVI RAJ GRUBB

I became Jacqueline du Pré's recording producer as a result of a casual remark I made on the occasion I heard her in person for the first time. It was on the evening of the last day of 1966; we were at a party to see the new year in, the 'we' including Daniel Barenboim. Jacqueline du Pré and Barenboim had met a few months earlier and the event which brought them together could not fairly be described as glamorous or romantic. Each had been laid low by a bout of glandular fever; when friends had mentioned du Pré's illness to Barenboim he had been sufficiently intrigued to telephone her and arrange for them to meet. They were instantly taken with each other and by December 1966 were constant companions. Wherever Barenboim is, sooner or later, there is bound to be music-making, and this evening was no exception. When we had all dined and wined the decks were cleared for the serious business of the evening and the proceedings were opened by du Pré and Barenboim. He asked her what she would like to play and in a tone of voice which suggested that there was only one work worthy of their collaboration she replied, '*The* Beethoven'. There was no need to say which of the Beethovens, for the emphasis on the definite article said it all, the Sonata in A major, op.69

They settled down and Barenboim gave her the 'A' and she tuned her instrument. I did not know then what a perfect sense of pitch du Pré has, but I did notice how very in tune she was with the piano. Having got the preliminaries out of the way, they looked at each other and du Pré launched the noble opening theme of op.69, one of Beethoven's great melodies. No one plays this soaring tune quite as

Jacqueline du Pré does – a suggestion of a slide from the first to the second note and a more distinct, but unexpected one between the A and the F sharp in the fourth bar, a slight swelling and dying away within the 'piano' asked for by Beethoven and the whole melody phrased in one long, arching line, shaped with the affection and tenderness demanded by the composer's marking, 'dolce'. As she reached the low E at the end of the phrase she turned to Barenboim almost as if to say: 'Match that, if you can', and with his delight plainly evident Barenboim responded to the challenge; it was a totally unrehearsed performance and one of the most notable I have heard of the work.

I had heard all the records du Pré had made till then and I knew the history of her astonishing career. My immediate reaction to her playing on records had been one of wonder that someone so young in years could produce music of this quality. Then had followed delight at her insight and instinctive feeling for the music of various periods she had recorded, and at the whole-hearted abandon of her playing. If at times this seemed a trifle excessive it was doubtless

With Sir John Barbirolli (right) and Suvi Raj Grubb, preparing to record the Haydn Cello Concerto in D major, 1967

due to the exuberance of youth; give me always over-enthusiasm rather than a chill remoteness. But the revelation of that evening for me was the sound of her cello heard face to face. Nothing I had heard on her records had prepared me for the singing tone of the instrument and for the sheer volume and opulence of the sound. I whispered to a colleague who was sitting next to me: 'We've not really captured that sound satisfactorily enough', and added, half jokingly, 'Bags I, her next recording.'

Less than four months later I welcomed Jacqueline du Pré to EMI's Abbey Road Studios in St John's Wood, London, as she arrived with Barenboim to make a record with the English Chamber Orchestra of Haydn's C major Cello Concerto and the well-known Boccherini B flat. We first set about the task of getting as natural a sound of the cello through the microphones as possible, subject only to the limitations of the medium. The first hurdle to be overcome for the successful recording of a cello is to ensure that it is not swamped by the accompaniment, whether an orchestra or a piano. It is played sitting down and is therefore on a level with the orchestral instruments. The groups of strings each outnumber the solo cello by at least six to one, the woodwind all have greater carrying power and the cello's range lies within that of some of the heaviest of the orchestral artillery: horns, trombones, bassoons and timpani.

To offset all this I set du Pré on a rostrum some nine inches high, thus raising her clear of the orchestra. Then we tried to find the best position for her in relation to the orchestra and we began with the natural one of her as at a concert, in front of the orchestra and facing away from it. She sounded marvellous but the leakage of the sound from the instruments more distant from her into her microphone made them go out of focus. I turned her around 180 degrees to face the orchestra. This sounded as if she and the English Chamber Orchestra were in, not two separate rooms, but two different towns. Then sideways, facing the conductor and so on till finally by a happy accident (and these things are always achieved by accident through trial and error and not through scientific calculation), I found the best position. I sat her plumb in the centre of the orchestra, facing the conductor, with the other players in a rough horseshoe around her. The conductor could have stretched out his hand and touched her and, wondering whether her proximity would cramp his movements, I asked him: 'Danny, is she too close?' His reply was a crisp: 'She can't ever be too close for me!'

Du Pré sat patiently and uncomplainingly through all this. When I asked her to play for a test she played out fully as she would have to an audience in a concert hall. When the recording began she played all out every time, as to a paying public. She never had the attitude: 'Oh well, if anything goes wrong we can always do it again.' This is one reason for the immediacy and vibrancy of her performances on gramophone records. Another is that she comes to recordings as thoroughly rehearsed and prepared as for a concert.

This recording once begun went very well and fast, for du Pré was in top form and responded joyously to the pains we had taken over the sound of her cello. Even a minor set-back – when she innocently changed her bow without telling anyone and drove us all to distraction trying to investigate all the possible causes for the sudden, inexplicable change in the sound of the cello before realizing that the new bow might have something to do with it and a little guiltily confessing – did not seriously retard progress. This, the first of her records I produced, provides a perfect example of her sense of style – classical propriety for the Haydn and romantic indulgence for the Boccherini.

The second record was also with Barenboim, of very different music, not so easy to perform or to balance, either for the players or for the recording team. The Brahms cello sonatas are probably the most superbly constructed of works for the two instruments, and the most difficult to bring off successfully. You cannot find two more incompatible instruments than the piano and the cello; besides, the cello's entire range lies within the compass of the piano's weightiest and most sonorous section and so when both are required to play loudly the pianist has to take special care not to swamp the cello. Brahms, of course, makes no concessions as far as the piano part is concerned, for it is as heavy and full as in a piano concerto. On the recording, to begin with, I did not set out to balance du Pré unduly prominently and thus make it easier for her to hold her own. This could be done later if necessary. I knew it would not be when she played the opening theme of the E minor and Barenboim's accompanying chords were played with the right degree of weight to support the cello and not drown it. I need not have worried even about the last movement of this sonata, a fugue. The contrapuntal lines were sharply etched whether on the cello or the piano. I marvelled at the musicianship of the two and the understanding between them which made each adjust the volume of sound to allow the important lines to come through. There is an

With Suvi Raj Grubb

eager spontaneity about these performances; du Pré and Barenboim
were still in the process of discovering each other and this is
reflected in their playing of these works.

Du Pré next visited the studios when Barenboim was recording
the Beethoven piano concertos with Klemperer. During one of the
intervals the conductor decided to find out for himself how much of
what he had heard of her phenomenal sense of pitch was justified.
He sat at the piano and played what could not possibly be described
as a chord, but was a weird combination of notes. 'Miss du Pré, what
notes am I playing?' he challenged and without even having to think
about it, she replied: 'A, B, C sharp, D sharp, F.' Klemperer himself
had to look down at the keyboard to confirm that she was right, and
having done that he said in admiration: 'So!' – a monosyllable he
could invest with greater meaning than most with an oration.

Hard on the heels of this she returned to record the Haydn D
major Concerto with one of her most ardent admirers, Sir John
Barbirolli. Barbirolli had a very special place in his heart for young
and enthusiastic musicians, and du Pré (and Barenboim) were

among the élite in his affections. When we were recording the Haydn, Evelyn Barbirolli visited us and as they were rehearsing leaned over to me and said: 'John is obviously having the time of his life', for over the cello you could hear him singing the opening theme of the concerto – this was always a mark of Barbirolli enjoying the music he was conducting.

Everyone who worked with du Pré in the recording studios adored her – the musicians who played with her, the conductor, or pianist who accompanied her, the engineers, the studio assistants and I. She was the ideal recording artist, undemanding, understanding of other people's problems and with no outbursts of what is called 'temperament', which all too often in the artistic world is a synonym for ill-humour. If her chair creaked or she wanted her music-stand raised, even before she asked for help, a watchful studio assistant would rush up with: 'Leave it all to me, Miss du Pré.' For the engineers she was the perfect artist who never complained however long it took to get the right sound through the microphones. For me, the all-too-brief six years in which we worked together are a golden memory of spontaneous, unaffected, joyous music-making. In the world of music it is rare for anyone to be universally liked and admired. It is always: 'So-and-so is a fine pianist, cellist or whatever, arguably the best around', and then the qualification: 'But of course . . .' often the retraction of the first part of the statement. Du Pré is one of possibly the only three artists I have known, about whom no one has ever said anything derogatory.

There was an interval of about six months between the Barbirolli record and the next one. Viewed in retrospect it seems such a great pity that we allowed all that time to elapse instead of cramming in as many records as we possibly could with her – but at the time no one dreamed that a finite limit had already been set on Jacqueline du Pré's musical career. No such thoughts clouded our minds in 1968 as we recorded the Schumann and Saint-Saëns concertos with the New Philharmonia Orchestra conducted by Barenboim. There was an even longer interval, over a year, between this and the next project. In five astonishing days astride New Year's Day, 1970, with Barenboim, Pinchas Zukerman and Gervaise de Peyer, she recorded all the Beethoven piano trios and variations for piano trio and the clarinet trio on five long-playing records. We recorded the 'Archduke' Trio last. When its last movement came to an end none of us knew that du Pré was to make only two more records – the illness which has laid her low physically but has left her spirit unbowed had already set its chill hand on her. One of the two was the Dvořák concerto with Barenboim in Chicago.

Even du Pré herself cannot pinpoint the exact time when she started experiencing mysterious and inexplicable symptoms such as a tingling in her fingers – a curious feeling of her hands and arms appearing, as she put it, to be made of lead – all these and a general malaise which seemed to drain all her energy. No one could yet explain what it was that ailed her, but she was at times so incapacitated as to have to cancel concerts and engagements, among them a long-cherished project of which I had high hopes. This was to record Schubert's 'Trout' Quintet with Perlman, Zukerman, Barenboim and a suitable double-bass player.

Early in December 1971, I had a telephone call from Barenboim. Was our Studio One free on 10 and 11 December? He explained that du Pré, who had not touched her cello for nearly six months, had a couple of days previously suddenly announced that she wanted to play. She had picked up her cello and Barenboim said had proceeded to play as if there had been no interval since she had last played. They had been running through the Chopin and Franck sonatas and he felt that she was playing as well as ever and perhaps we should try and record these works. I was delighted and made all the necessary arrangements. In those two days we completed the recording. There was no sign of her illness and she played as superbly as always. When we had finished she said she would like to start on the Beethoven sonatas. Barenboim and I were concerned, for she looked tired, but we recorded the first movement of op.5, No 1. At the end of it she placed her cello back in its case with: 'That is that', and did not even want to listen to what we had taped. That was Jacqueline du Pré's last appearance in the recording studio.

In 1973, the illness was at last given its dread name, and in me, as I am sure in the hearts of all who know and love her, there was an anguished cry of: 'Oh, no!'

What was it that made Jacqueline du Pré so special an artist and which makes her loss to music so unbearable? I would place in the forefront her total mastery of her instrument. The cello is basically an intractable instrument. Its very size makes it difficult to control. It requires strong muscles to handle it and to coax a beguiling sound from it. When du Pré walked on to a stage or into a recording room with her instrument, one's immediate impression was that the cello was an extension of herself. She carried it and handled it easily and comfortably. She is tall and well-built and this contributed to the ease with which she played.

Her technical mastery of the cello was absolute. The tone she produced was rich and sonorous, always in a long singing line and she had an astonishing capacity to colour it with the most delicate shades. It could be dark and foreboding for the opening theme of Brahms's E minor Sonata, impassioned in the first theme of Beethoven's op.69, with a jaunty lilt in the last movement of the Dvořák, wistful and a trifle sad for the slow middle section of the Lalo, or whatever matched the mood of the music. She had an instinctive feeling for the emotional content of any music she played and so had the ability to get to its heart.

She was an unselfish player and so was an ideal partner in chamber music. And added to all this was a sheer delight in making music. You could see this in the smiles she exchanged with other players and the nods with which she acknowledged someone playing a passage especially well. She has often said to me that she hated practising and I have never arrived at her house to find her practising. Playing music, yes, but not scales or arpeggios or exercises. I cannot explain how, in view of this, at concerts and recordings the notes came so easily to her fingers and how she worked out the strongly individual interpretations which charac-terize her work – but then, you cannot explain genius and if I were allowed to apply that term to only one of the many musicians I have worked with, it would be to Jacqueline du Pré.

My Dearest Friend
by
EUGENIA ZUKERMAN

Since we first met in 1967, Jackie has been my dearest friend and much like a sister to me. Soon after the musical collaboration between Pinky, Daniel and Jackie began, having all become close friends, we decided to take a holiday together, of which I have most vivid recollections. It was August 1968 and we went to the Hebrides. We stayed on the Island of Mull and frequently Jackie and I would go for walks and climb the hills together. For such activities the men did not show any particular enthusiasm. On our many rambles I found it necessary to make quite considerable efforts to keep up with Jackie; she was so full of energy and would walk so fast. She was always full of joy and appreciation when walking in a brisk wind and was absolutely amazed at the rugged beauty of the place. There were moments when I thought of her as some sort of golden bird flying over those hills. I remember experiencing great surges of love for her.

At that time she was not enormously intellectual but I felt there was a tremendous intelligence and a most intuitive mind at work; a very clear, vivid and uncluttered mind, unaffected by much academic schooling. So, as we talked during our long walks, there could be no intellectual discussions, yet in our conversations it soon became clear she had her own very private, very personal and very gentle philosophy about life. After that holiday, when she and I had spent so much time together in that primitive landscape, I was aware that a strong bond had developed between us.

Then, of course, there was the joy of hearing and seeing her in performance. Pinky, Danny and she became a most successful trio and wanted to be able to play together as frequently as possible. There were several tours and I would always go along with them. Discounting the fact of my great personal affection for Jackie, I would sit there like any other member of the audience and find that I was being completely dazzled by her playing. It was so touching to see this tall, striking girl with the flowing blonde hair come onto the platform rather like Alice in Wonderland, sit down and wrap herself around the cello. The music she produced was so intensely direct, so incredibly emotional, so utterly personal that you, the listener, felt that she was speaking individually to you through that instrument.

From 1968 until her illness I was fortunate in being her frequent travelling companion, not only when the trio was performing, but when she was giving recitals. On one occasion, when she was playing in Oklahoma City, she had an inkling something was wrong. I recall her saying to me: 'I only have strength when I play the cello. I can hardly open a window or fasten my suitcase.' That, I think, was when she was first becoming aware of something disabling happening to her body. As the early seventies progressed it seemed to me her artistry was increasing and reaching tremendous

Reg Wilson

A joyous moment as husband accompanies wife in
September 1967

Reg Wilson

heights. Then, when she was at the top of her form, there was nothing like it. Never have I heard anything comparable before or since, recorded or in the concert hall. It was a passion she was able to share; a form of selfless giving; a deep belief in and a commitment to the music. Just watching Jackie play was a treat in itself, always without inhibitions, so unpretentious and totally spontaneous.

When she became ill all her close friends felt involved in the calamity and as it became clear that, at least for a while, she would be unable to play the cello, there was a terrible sense of loss which one shared with her. What was most striking about the way Jackie reacted to the discovery of her illness was her frankness; she made no attempt to delude herself or those close to her. Yet in everything she said and did there was a great dignity. I am sure her secret was that she did not resign herself to her illness and most certainly still does not do so. Nor indeed do her friends, because there is always the chance that at any moment her condition may be reversed.

As a person Jackie is still as she always was, the same cheerful, unfettered soul. In fact, perhaps because the performance of music is no longer possible, other aspects of her magical personality began to develop and her interests have rapidly increased. She has discovered books, poetry and the theatre. Far from feeling sorry for herself she steeps herself in these things and has learned a great deal from them. Instead of the quick, clever, intuitive girl I first knew, she has become highly self-educated; a new, changed and mature Jackie. And the change is really quite staggering. For instance, I find that, when reading poetry, she is far better able than anyone I know quickly to grasp the full meaning of a phrase. This may well be due to her musical ability, enabling her immediate recognition of a statement profoundly expressed.

Jackie has in fact become a talisman – a symbol of hope and encouragement – for other multiple sclerosis sufferers. It is only reasonable to consider that she has lost more than the average person contracting the illness. She was, I think, aware of the extent of her gift. That she is not bitter and has overcome so much by being perpetually active and helpful to others is deserving of great praise indeed. She is one of the most original women I have ever known.

Sensuous Sound

by

PINCHAS ZUKERMAN

I first heard about Jackie in 1965 from Charles Wadsworth, who was then director of the chamber concerts at the Spoleto Festival. He told me he had met this fantastic cellist and he believed that if the two of us ever got together it would be a match made in heaven. So the name Jacqueline du Pré not unnaturally was firmly fixed in my mind. And, as if this was not enough, later that year I heard from Arnold Steinhardt, of the Guarneri Quartet, that they had, in fact, been playing at Spoleto with this girl and he talked to me at great length about what an extraordinary musician she was. Finally my wife, Genie, and I went round back stage after a concert in New York and at last met Jackie. As we stood chatting, Daniel said to me, 'Look, why don't you come around tomorrow and we can play some trios at Essex House?' I said that would be fine with me. As it happened I was not doing anything at the time, so I took my fiddle along and we all three played. I thought we would just play a movement or so, but as we made music together the rapport between us was quite incredible. It was without doubt the most extraordinary thing that has ever happened to me. To have another player to whom it is unnecessary to say a thing, who, by a look, a movement of an arm, can understand the slightest nuance; for me this was something quite unique in communication. It was also something which I strongly suspect is never likely to happen to me again.

Most great string players have their own particular sound. It is what might be called a 'personality sound' and belongs to the particular player exclusively. Jackie had her own unique sound in abundance. My description of it would be to call it sensuous. It is a facet of playing which I find extremely difficult to describe. It is something one hears and immediately recognizes: when the player brings out a particular note or phrase in a special way. It was for Jackie absolutely instinctive musicality and few people have this great gift. (I believe today Pavarotti is similarly fortunate in having this instinct and I understand that at one time he did not even read music.) Jackie had an extraordinary physical ability with the cello. Fingering presented absolutely no problems for her; it was as if she was born holding a finger board. There are not a great number of players I can recall with such a facility. Yehudi Menuhin had the gift in his early years, Michael Raeburn, Horowitz . . . It is an ability that string players constantly pursue and is for most of them maddeningly elusive.

Everything about Jackie in performance was completely natural and spontaneous. Sometimes people will ask why she made those flourishes with the bow. I am frequently asked why I 'dance' when I play. It is just a part of the natural and instinctive movement of the body; one has no conscious realization that one is doing it. The flourishes were something that was a part of Jackie's normal reaction when playing the instrument. Certainly it was no affectation or façade. Of course, for some people's tastes such mannerisms may appear at times to be exaggerated, but that is no matter because an instrumentalist will do it with absolute conviction and feeling.

There could be a sense of being slightly left in the shadows when appearing on the same concert platform with Jackie. One had somehow to pull out of the shadows and try to match up to what was happening. You must never fight such a situation; you go along with it and you may well discover that you are being taken along on a marvellous ride. It is a quite tremendous feeling. When we were playing trios Jackie always had the sensitivity and ability to listen to what I was doing. Never was it ever a case of her wishing to establish herself as the focal player; her concern was always for the trio as a unit – ever a matter of give and take. She had an uncanny personality on the platform, partly because of the way she looked and partly because of the way she played. The general impression was of a person completely inspired in delivering a message of the greatest possible importance to the audience.

When we all four travelled together we had great times; there were always lots of giggles and a great deal of laughter. Jackie has a

great instinct for fun and a well developed sense of the ridiculous, so anybody with the slightest tendency towards pomposity has to beware. She is such a happy person with an outstandingly kind and sweet nature, in fact I know one of her friends always calls her 'Smiley'. I cannot recall a single instance of her ever getting angry, although, like so many great talents, there are times when she can be just a trifle absent-minded.

Since her illness Jackie, of course, has had more time for reflection and she has devoted a great deal of it to considering fully the technique of playing the cello. We have had a number of chats about stopping, bowing and the various other facets of execution; she has clearly given considerable thought to this and done a great deal of reading about the subject. Happily it is a subject in which she can still be involved with all the tremendous practical benefits to be derived from her instinct, talent and experience.

Let me say now that there is not the slightest sign from her of bitterness about her illness, which might reasonably have been expected from an artist whose brilliant career is so suddenly and arbitrarily halted. Her dedication and love of music have been maintained and she still very much wants to be involved. It seems to me that perhaps it would be a good idea if Jackie could be encouraged to write about her feelings today: the way she views music and the musical world. It would be of immense help and guidance to other musicians who might find themselves in a similar situation and, of course, it would provide fascinating reading for all music lovers, not to mention the countless fans who have so much enjoyed Jackie's great talent.

A Film Called 'Jacqueline'
by
CHRISTOPHER NUPEN

There are just a few in any generation, musicians with the unmistakable qualities that make the rare but familiar figure of the internationally acclaimed artist.

It is one of the most totally absorbing of all professions, demanding not only great fantasy and the god-given talent to communicate, but the character and will to develop it and an essential single-mindedness from the earliest age.

The demands are high and are met by just a few. At twenty-two Jacqueline du Pré is already among them.

Those words emerged from a flurry of activity and considerable excitement as the opening commentary to a film called *Jacqueline* which we made for the BBC in much too much of a hurry in 1967. We were given just under three weeks to make a film about what I felt at the time was the finest cello talent on earth. I may have been wrong about this, but the conviction did a great deal to get us through. How do you even start to make a film that would do justice to Jacqueline du Pré? It would have been difficult enough in three months and we were both young and dangerously inexperienced; but youth has its advantages. We shot a sixty-five minute film in less than three weeks and edited it in six, and happily it succeeded none the less in capturing something of her magical qualities.

Films are made in the editing, but they depend absolutely on what happens in front of the camera during the filming. In those three weeks Jackie, who had never made a film before, strode gaily in front of the camera with that curious combination of shyness and absolute conviction that have characterized her personality since her teens. The camera liked what it saw. She was full of youthful, burning eagerness and fortunately the camera sees such things very clearly.

My conviction that there was no finer cellist on earth obviously had much to do with my affection for her, but the enjoyment of music is a strange thing. There are doubtless better reasons for adopting convictions of this kind, and certainly my enthusiasm to communicate the idea landed me in hot water on more than one occasion with distinguished professionals who knew much more about these things than I did. But how can one argue with that overpowering personal response that some performances can evoke? Some may find the extremes of her fantasy rather heady stuff, but in John Barbirolli's words, 'I love it!'

Sir John was in the middle of recording Vaughan Williams's *Sea Pictures* at the Abbey Road Studios when we asked him if there was anything that he would like to say about Jackie for the film. He paid her as profound a tribute as one could expect from one artist to another, and he concluded with, 'You know, she is sometimes now accused of excessive emotions and things. But I love it. When you are young, you should have an excess of everything. If you haven't an excess when you are young, what are you going to pare off as the years go by? Such heaven-sent gifts don't appear every day.' The years pared off more than any of us dreamed possible and I am profoundly grateful for having been so close to so many of those excessive concerts and so much under the magic of the spells that she was able to weave.

The intervening years and listening to both studio and concert recordings have done nothing to diminish my wonder at her playing. Her command of the instrument and her intonation were on a level that few could match, but there was so much more to it than that. The confidence and sure-footedness in her phrasing which gave her such freedom; her ability to respond to the moment and her apparent total lack of inhibition; these are qualities that she seems to share more with musicians of the past than the present. And there is something else, a miraculous combination of apparently contradictory qualities. She had the ability to phrase with such natural conviction as to give the impression that it really should not be done in any other way, and at the same time to make you catch your breath with surprise and delight at an unexpected sound or turn in the phrase. All so natural that it could not be otherwise and yet so surprising that life could suddenly take on a

Reg Wilson

Rehearsing Schubert's 'Trout' quintet, August 1969, L to R: Itzhak Perlman, Daniel Barenboim, Jackie, Zubin Mehta on the double bass, Pinchas Zukerman. The performance of the 'Trout' was the only time this group of friends worked together

new dimension for a few seconds. To my ears this is a quality that she shares with very few. I think of Caruso, Lotte Lehmann, Andrés Segovia, the young Menuhin or the young Zukerman. How do you explain it? You cannot, but in Jackie's case the apparent contradictions are curiously reminiscent of the shy determination of her personality.

Hagiography? Why not? Our liberal age seems to have more than its fair share of inhibitions and taboos about these things. In many ways Jackie's playing seemed to be the very antidote of inhibition; perhaps because she suffered so much from the effects of it in her childhood. I still shudder at the memory of her account of a pubescent Jacqueline du Pré having to endure the profound affront of schoolmates dancing around her chanting, 'We hate Jackie', and all because nature had endowed her with such prodigious gifts.

Most musicians seem to acquire their best qualities with the passage of time; as much by experience and in response to what their public demands of them as by native talent. But to my ears Jackie seemed to arrive almost fully fledged, with most of her unique qualities virtually intact. Even her idiosyncrasies seemed in some way to form a natural part of a complete musical personality. She was often advised by wiser colleagues in rehearsal to omit some of these in the coming performance; in particular what she now refers to as her 'sumptuous glissandi'. She would agree shyly, modify the rehearsal accordingly and then re-introduce them in the performance with a combination of childlike glee and ferocious determination that would make the effect succeed after all.

I recall one such occasion when I was present at the rehearsal but missed the concert and she later informed me that she had done it in the evening anyway. 'How was it?' I asked. 'Gorgeous!' came the reply. As Daniel Barenboim says in the *Jacqueline* film, 'It is all so natural with her, and comes so much from inside, that you can't help loving it. But those of us who have to conduct, of course, find it sometimes rather hard.'

I first heard Jackie's playing on a BBC Third Programme relay of a solo Bach recital from Fenton House on a summer evening. I had never heard the name Jacqueline du Pré and suddenly she transformed the night into some sort of velvety magic that still echoes somewhere in my memory. Soon afterwards she strode shyly, as was her way, into the flat which I shared with John Williams at the time. They were preparing an arrangement for cello and guitar of Manuel de Falla's *Jota* for her first recording with EMI. She was fifteen years old. I was captured, and have admired and loved her ever since, as much for her incorruptibility and her originality as for her playing.

After making the *Jacqueline* film, which has fortunately been preserved, we made a number of television programmes together for the BBC, all of which have sadly been destroyed. I then left the Corporation largely because I had realized in the making of the *Jacqueline* film that such things could not really be done properly within the unavoidable limitations of the large television stations. Then in 1969 we made *The Trout* as an independent production, when Itzhak Perlman, Pinchas Zukerman, Jacqueline du Pré, Zubin Mehta and Daniel Barenboim played Schubert's Trout Quintet in the Queen Elizabeth Hall one August afternoon. This was arranged by Barenboim as part of London's first season of South Bank Summer Music. We filmed the concert live, on stage, exactly as it happened and without retakes, having followed the preparations and rehearsals at extremely close quarters during the preceding five days.

Until that time chamber music had been thought of as at best suitable for late-night television, but the combination of youthful exuberance and passionate dedication which radiated from the performers, the way in which they related and adapted to each other both in rehearsal and in the performance, and which, once again the camera saw very clearly, made the resulting film probably the most frequently televised classical music programme to date.

We had only one more opportunity to put Jackie's playing on film before her illness began to affect her playing. During 1970 I had heard the Barenboim-Zukerman-du Pré trio play Beethoven's Piano Trio op.70, No. 1 ('The Ghost') in Oxford and Brighton. Their performances were like nothing I had ever heard and left me with the impression that 'The Ghost' was a mightier trio than the 'Archduke'. A few days later we were to have made a film with Andrés Segovia in St John's, Smith Square, London, which had to be cancelled only two days before the event. St John's was booked, needless to say, and the trio was in Brighton and happened to have a free day. They came to London by train early in the morning and went back again by the last train that night, leaving behind them something at least of their miraculous performances on film. Years later, after a viewing of the film, I was lamenting the fact that no film could ever hope to capture properly the extraordinary atmosphere of those concerts in Oxford and Brighton. 'Nonsense,' was Jackie's immediate response. 'It's better on the film. To be able to see what's going on like that adds another dimension.' She was wrong, of course, but such is her uninhibited pleasure in her music-making, and her generosity. That remark also reflects something of the gratitude that both of us feel at having had the unexpected opportunity to preserve something of her playing on film.

Until her illness began to transform her attitude to the world, Jackie was regarded by many who knew her well as a rather fay but blithe spirit who knew little or nothing of worldly things and, in a way, she was just that. She often had no idea what day it was or when or where her next concert might be. She certainly had little idea of what things cost. But her perception of the true nature of things and people was always rock solid and ran extremely deep. This quality has actually deepened with her illness, although it has become less sure-footed because of her desperate need to replace some of the affection that was once lavished on her by thousands of admirers. She misses that.

Reg Wilson

Recording a Beethoven trio at the EMI studios, December 1969:
Zukerman, Barenboim and du Pré

Her awareness of suffering has deepened too. Small wonder! Anyone watching and hearing her performance of the Elgar Concerto in the *Jacqueline* film would be likely to think that her projection of Elgar's melancholy could hardly have deepened with the passage of time. I doubt it myself, because I have always thought that in some strange way it was directly related to her youth; a curious combination of youthful sensitivity, uninhibited energy and musical honesty. But to see her lately, sitting in front of an Elgar photograph that hangs in her living-room, and musing about his melancholy as she feels it in his music now, makes me wonder what she would convey to *us* now, if her strength and her co-ordination should be given back to her.

To reflect on these things is to tread close to the brink of hell; and there is another thought that torments me. For years Jackie and my wife, who was also known by her professional name, Diana Baikie, were the closest and most intimate of friends. They had many qualities in common, among them a respect for nature and for all things on the earth. They never knowingly hurt anyone or anything and never mistreated themselves or anyone else. Indeed, they always brought the best out in others. Why nature should so mistreat them in return is an awesome and unfathomable mystery.

Diana died at the age of thirty-nine and Jacqueline du Pré has to suffer the miseries of multiple sclerosis. In the words of Andrés Segovia, speaking out of the most profound affection for them both, 'I do not understand, and never will, the cruelty of nature.' And yet their capacity to struggle bravely, and Jackie's efforts to transcend her appalling loss, are the most touching things that I have ever witnessed. Her attitude was perfectly summed up in a BBC programme which took for its title her spontaneous phrase, 'I really am a very lucky person.' To understand something of the dialectic of those two phrases in all their profundity is to go some way to understanding the mystery of Jacqueline du Pré.

Jackie's Master Classes
by
SIR IAN HUNTER

Jacqueline du Pré came to Harold Holt Limited in 1967, soon after she married Daniel Barenboim, whose debut in this country we had arranged in 1955 when he was twelve years old, and whose career we have looked after ever since. It seemed sensible that as they performed together so often they should have the same management to co-ordinate their complicated schedules.

But it is not as an agent but rather as a Festival Director or entrepreneur that I want to write about Miss du Pré. She was a wonderful artist with whom to work, always warm and enthusiastic and ready to enter into the spirit of the event. At the first Brighton Festival in 1967 she gave a recital in the exotic Music Room of the Royal Pavilion, later to be badly damaged by fire, and a performance of the Boccherini concerto in the Dome. In 1968 she came again, and gave the world première of a work we had commissioned for her from Alexander Goehr, 'Romanza for Cello and Orchestra', with the Philharmonia conducted by Daniel. She was well aware of the need to increase the orchestral repertory for the cello and she made light of the technical difficulty of the work.

Two years later, in the Church of the Holy Sepulchre, as part of the City of London Festival, she gave a performance of three Bach suites for unaccompanied cello – an evening of unique spirituality which will never be forgotten by those who heard it. In the vestry before the recital began I found her telling a joke and saying, 'I really mustn't be irreverent', whilst at the same time drawing sonorous chords from her cello as she tuned the instrument. Like so many colleagues of her generation she can move from complete relaxation

Reg Wilson

Barenboim and du Pré at work

to deep concentration in the time it takes to get to the stage.

As her playing career reached its height with a performance of the Elgar concerto conducted by Zubin Mehta at the Royal Festival Hall in February 1973 shortly followed by an American tour, her illness became apparent and whilst Daniel was in Israel at the time of the Yom Kippur War in the autumn of that year, it was diagnosed. There are many who will tell better than I of her fortitude during those days but I remember vividly how cheerfully she had accepted the limitations her illness had imposed on her when I visited her in St Mary's Hospital, Paddington. Then she and Daniel moved to Knightsbridge and it became easier for us to see her and to talk. To talk, to plan and for her to try out on her friends words of which she had just discovered the meaning in her dictionary. She seemed fascinated by learning and poetry. 'I was taken away from school when I was twelve and now I am making up for lost time.'

It was during these talks that she began discussing teaching, and various people were brought in to advise. We thought it would be

Reg Wilson

wonderful if she could be persuaded to give Master Classes and I told Daniel that I would happily invite her to start with two classes at the Brighton Festival in 1977. Gradually the idea was advanced and Erica Klien was to undertake the organization of pupils and classes.

When 9 July 1977 arrived Jackie and Daniel motored down from London and we went to lunch at Wheeler's Restaurant on the front where we had in earlier days had suppers with Artur Rubinstein after his concerts which Daniel had conducted; the pair of them told stories far into the night. Jackie seemed in fine form and we had lobster and white wine – I think I also had something stronger to steady my nerves because neither Daniel nor I was at all sure how Jackie would react to appearing before the public again. As she was wheeled onto the platform at the Polytechnic Theatre there was a great wave of applause and the artist in her immediately responded. The Master Class began and everyone was at ease. I was amazed that someone to whom music came so naturally was able to put into words so explicitly her criticisms and appreciation without recourse to demonstrating on the cello. There were many memorable remarks: 'Barbirolli told me to listen for the bass lead,' she said of one moment in the Elgar concerto which was being studied.

Although her health was uneven she taught regularly and in June 1978 I invited her to repeat her Elgar Master Class at the Malvern Festival which is held in the small Worcestershire town where Elgar lived and was buried. Again she had a great success and enjoyed the associations remaining with the great English composer of whose concerto she must surely stand as one of the greatest and most idiomatic interpreters.

Master Classes at the South Bank Festival in London, organized by her friend and colleague Pinchas Zukerman, followed in August 1979, and during the spring and summer of that year BBC TV made programmes which were later to be seen by millions. Many great artists have given Master Classes over the years but those of Jacqueline du Pré are unique in that she has but her speech, her hands and her personality to project to both pupil and audience the musical interpretations which are the essence of her art.

Absolute Beginner
by
JAMES D. WOLFENSOHN

I shall always remember Jackie on those Sunday afternoons in the early seventies, when at forty I took my first cello lessons. After she had been diagnosed as having multiple sclerosis and her concert career was in doubt, I had dined with Daniel and Jackie and we discussed her future – she would teach – but who would be her first student? I volunteered, half in jest, half in hope that she would accept me. She called me at my office the next day to tell me that she had arranged a cello for me with the renowned dealer, Charles Beare, and our two-year adventure began.

As I am a banker, midweek lessons were not possible, so each Sunday afternoon we met. Nervously, I would attempt to tune my instrument, trying to judge from Jackie's eyes and from my untrained ears whether I was sharp or flat. She will never know what a trauma it was for me just getting ready to start playing.

I would take out my work for the week, assigned by her from compositions she had played when she was six, seven or eight years old. At the beginning, I played simple pieces written for her by her Mother and illustrated to attract a child's interest, but this was only briefly, and we were soon into Bach, Fauré and Saint-Saëns.

Never did Jackie make me feel inadequate. She would encourage me when by chance I made a reasonable sound or phrase. I would treasure her 'bravos'. When more often my tone and pitch were poor, she would encourage me to try again. While physically able to do so, she would show me how to draw the bow or to move the hand on the fingerboard, but as her condition prevented such demonstration, she would show me in other ways. She would motion with her

Reg Wilson

hands in time with her music. She would count for me. She would
gesture with a sweep of her arms above her head to describe the
climax of a phrase. And she would sing, and she would breathe – for
string playing is like singing. She would sorrow with its mood. And
we would talk of the essence of the music and of the life it portrayed.

I played 'The Swan' for weeks and months. A dozen times she
would explain a phrase and the bowings and where to place the bow
in relation to the bridge. I could understand, but how difficult it was
to follow her instructions. For then, as now, my control of the
instrument was limited and without basic technical training, and
without those young hours of scales and exercises, my dreams of
artistic accomplishment were unfulfilled.

Maybe it would have been better if Jackie and I had spent our first
months with scales and with explanations of the positions of the
hands, going through the tedium of beginning string players. But
that was not her way. We started with complex compositions, for
Jackie believed I could learn through playing and it would be more
fun. She had never taught a beginner before – and I fear after her
experience with me – not since. I cannot believe she was ever a

beginner herself. To her, playing is a natural gift. She gave me a photo at the age of seven drawing a bow with perfect form on a cello almost as big as she. Our sessions revolved around the music; the technique would come from playing and with practice. She wanted me to feel the music, and to learn as she had done, by playing. I am still studying a decade later, now living and working in New York. My technique still suffers, but what Jackie gave me was a far greater gift. It was the unique illumination of music through her eyes, through her ears, through her heart.

In yet another quite different way Jackie has influenced my life and that of thousands of others.

Nearly six years ago I was invited to become President of the International Federation of Multiple Sclerosis Societies, which has twenty national groups around the world, devoted to the care and assistance of MS persons and to research into the causes of the baffling disease. My sole claim to this position was my affection for and friendship with Jackie, and it is to her that I have devoted my work in these recent years. Throughout the world we have highly competent and selfless professional staff, backed by amateurs such as I, of whom many, many more are needed.

So many of us wander around ignoring or shutting our eyes to disabilities in any form; and I was no exception. Happily I now no longer adopt this attitude. MS has never been a 'glamorous' complaint, embraced by outstanding public generosity. Contributory reasons for this are incorrect diagnosis and ignorance of the disease or failure to face up to it by patients or their families.

When I was elected President I decided that we needed to increase both public awareness of MS and the level of research into the causes of the disease. Jackie was in complete agreement with these objectives. Daniel had already gathered together a loose consortium of his musical colleagues who agreed to offer their services in an endeavour to raise funds for MS. It was Daniel's lead, together with my election as President of the International Federation, which enabled us to establish formally a group of celebrities who would give concerts to help in raising much-needed resources throughout the world. It was decided to establish the Jacqueline du Pré Research Fund.

Since we began four years ago we have held a number of concerts in the United Kingdom, the USA, Canada, Denmark, France, Israel and elsewhere. More are planned. We gave a special benefit performance with many great dancers at Covent Garden; then there was Pinky Zukerman and the English Chamber Orchestra in New York, with performances elsewhere by many, including Ashkenazy, Misha and Cipa Dichter, Zubin Mehta and by Daniel himself, many times.

All this has done two things: it has, of course, raised a considerable amount of money, but what is far more important is that it has made a worldwide public aware of MS.

By becoming more widely known, MS is now attracting scientists to study the all-important research issues. People are also becoming more aware that it is possible to face MS courageously and to lead a fulfilling life within the context of the world's disabled.

I think the way Jackie, a pre-eminent performer and still a pre-eminent musician, has been able to adjust her life has given tremendous help to others. Jackie, in some strange way, has exchanged the recognition she was accorded as a musical virtuoso for a similar acknowledgement in adversity. She has made the transition with great bravery and sensitivity, and with cost to her privacy and with strain on her physical condition. She is a symbol throughout the world and an inspiration to the thousands of MS persons who daily show their determination to lead normal lives within their physical limitation.

I cannot end this brief tribute to Jackie without mention of Daniel, whose patience, understanding and support have enabled her to manage her life so splendidly. His courage and insight in facing all the inherent problems have had a profound impact on everyone who knows him.

Jackie was born for greatness. First as a musician and now as a symbol and inspiration for MS persons has she become renowned. But it is Jackie as a human being, luminous, loving, full of insight and emotion that I feel privileged to know and to call her my friend – and my teacher.

Jackie and the Wolf
by
JANET SUZMAN

She's got this really dirty laugh, unexpected in one so blonde, a gurgling giggle and dazzling grin which makes you feel positively better than you did a moment before. So when the full force of all this disarming battery is turned on you, you tend to succumb. Even over the telephone it's pretty powerful stuff, and combined as it was with a suspiciously meek request to please come and help her with *Peter and the Wolf*, well, naturally, I succumbed. Off I went to teach my grandmother to suck eggs. This, by the way, was a few years ago when she first ventured onto the stage in this new capacity of raconteuse.

One thing was absolutely clear to me as I drove to her house: her muscles may be ravaged by this ghastly, unfair illness she has contracted, but her instinct remains as clear and pure and strong as ever it was. There was not going to be much I could teach her. We sat in the drawing-room, her score on her knees, while she read the story to me, every now and then whistling the music of it, which clearly was easier for her to read than the words. She read it with an almost childlike freshness which was so utterly right that I found I could say nothing of any helpfulness whatsoever, just as I expected I wouldn't. I've heard some Peter and the Wolfers adopt a slightly condescending tone as if to signal 'children's story'; this affectation eluded her, much to my delight. So apart from feebly pointing out that maybe she was inclined to lean a little too firmly on the odd past participle ('no sooner HAD Peter gone than . . .'), we left the work alone and had tea.

Listening to her, something struck me as charmingly paradoxical,

Jackie by Zsuzsi Roboz

which is that her most Gallic of names seems by osmosis to have crept unwittingly into her speech, for although her French is no more than passing good, she appears to have the slightest touch of it in her otherwise frightfully English English. The merest hint of something foreign slips in and out of her speech like a spy disguising his origins. I can't put my finger on exactly where it crops up, but it gives to her speaking a most particular ring.

Music is life, breath, food and inspiration to her; the element she swims in like a lovely trout. The rockier waters of the word-spouter are more strange to her. She forsakes her usual musical elegance and that fierce frown of concentration and becomes endearingly like a puppy splashing in a mud bath. She didn't have much schooling and so her literary education is astonishingly zero, but that's one of the many things that makes me love her. What a relief it is to a person whose daily business is words, words and more words, to talk to someone whose response to them is immediate and fresh and uncluttered by a boring old education. She has no prejudices of a literary kind, no half-formed ideas; she is exhilaratingly unread, a tabula positively rasa! She hasn't even heard of *Gone with the Wind*, for heaven's sake! It tends to make one think about things all over again.

Musicians seem to me to trust their talents as a baby does its mother; they believe in the miraculous nature of music as a mother does her baby. Actors are far more suspicious of their talents; they disbelieve their powers, tussle with meanings and styles; in short they mistrust themselves an awful lot of the time. But, still, there is at least one thing that performers have in common: timing. If you have it, you have it. No one can teach you that elusive and priceless sense of what is right. Jackie has that thing in abundance, plus the most finely tuned ear that ever sat in a head. So is it any wonder that when I went to see my famous 'protégée' do her stuff at the Purcell Room, I should have preened with vicarious pride? Not a trick was missed in Peter's adventures with the wolf and assorted other animals; the delicacy with which she lauded the excessive bravery of the duck quacking angrily at the cat 'from the *middle* of the pond'; the mournful reverberations of nasty duck fate contained in '. . . and with one gulp *swallowed* her'; the infant braggadocio expressed in 'boys such as he were not afraid of *wolves*'; the cautious exactitude of self-preservation in ' . . . not *too* close to the cat'.

And who says she doesn't have an ear for the collective clout of the compounded consonant? No one has reached such depths of disdain with 'what kind of bird are you if you can't SSWIMM and DDIVVED into the pond', or such green-eyed viciousness with those crazy foreign r's of hers growling 'GRRABB' and 'GRREEEDY'. 'Imagine the TRYUMphant prrocession!' cried Jackie as this little jewel of musical story-telling trod brightly to its end, the laughs coming unerringly and sweetly, lovingly conducted by Daniel towards that equally TRYUMphant figure in her wheelchair. Is there no end to her talents, I ask myself? Endowed with a quite sublime musical talent, she now shows dangerous signs of becoming a first-rate comedienne.

Press Association

After receiving the OBE, February 1976

'I Was Lucky, You See'
by
JACQUELINE DU PRÉ

(Compiled from conversations with the Editor and from BBC
television and radio programmes)

The very first time I heard a cello was on the radio in a programme
for children to show them every instrument in the orchestra. I
remember telling my mother: 'I want one of those please.' I was
four. It was managed in a rather magical way. I woke up one
morning and there was a cello beside the bed. It was with very great
excitement that I took it up and tried it. My mother fostered my
enthusiasm for the instrument by writing pieces for me. To the
music she put words and drawings, she would tell me the rhyme or
the words, show me the drawings and by that time I loved it so much
that playing was the greatest delight. I remember being inspired
later by the idea of horse hair and cat gut (well actually sheep gut)
getting together to make that lovely sound. In fact I still remember
hearing somewhere, 'A noise rose from the orchestra as the leader
drew the tail of the noble horse across the intestines of the timid
cat.'

When I was three I ran away from home. I was missing from seven
in the morning until seven-thirty in the evening and the police were
alerted. I did it again when I was five – on my tricycle.

At school I was one of those children who was made a scapegoat.
It was never easy for me to join in. Being rather miserable and feeling
isolated, when I actually left school it was a welcome day. I loved
maths. I loved English; I think much education can be acquired
without necessarily having it in a formalized manner. The way one
does perhaps lose out is through not being with other people and
therefore not learning to adjust with them and learning about life
with them.

When my family lived in Portland Place my father had a stick insect – bless its heart. But I could find no way to love it . . . I hated it. She was named Amanda – Mandy for short – and lived in her own aquarium. When she died she was given a burial in nearby Regent's Park. A deeply religious service was conducted by my father, who still remembers the spot where Amanda lies.

My first real public appearance in 1961 at the Wigmore Hall was memorable in more ways than one. After beginning the first piece, which was the Handel G minor Sonata, the A string began to unwind itself. This meant the sound got lower and lower. To compensate for this I was obliged to go higher and higher up the keyboard until the string finally fell to the floor. It happened very slowly, so that the audience did not realize what was happening. When it finally dropped it was obvious that I could not go on playing. By the time I had changed the string and was back on stage, there had been a few moments for reflection and I went back actually feeling stronger than when I started.

I loved performing. An audience consists of a variety of people, so there is no particular person or persons one has to play to, but every audience has its own particular aura. Every concert feels entirely different, the audience reaction is both interesting and stimulating. And it is possible to speak most eloquently through music.

I was used to being alone on my travels. I would read or explore the city I was in, but what I didn't like was going down to a big restaurant in a hotel, sitting down at a table alone. So I would eat in my room.

The cello is a lonely instrument and it needs another instrument or an orchestra with a conductor. So that to achieve a complete fulfilment from what one is doing, it is necessary to have someone with whom one has a great bond musically. It happened very frequently for me with my husband.

My first meeting with my husband was most remarkable. The door was opened and in came this very dynamic person; he sat down and we played through something, and to my surprise there was nothing to say, it was as though we had known each other for a very long time. It was a wonderful feeling. Sometimes I might not chat with someone as easily as I would wish, but with a fellow musician and somebody I liked, I knew I would be able to talk very freely, through music.

When Daniel went to Israel in 1967, I was pretty frightened and wanted to be with him. There was no war for ten days and we spent

Rehearsing Haydn's Toy Symphony at the Royal Albert Hall, July 1979. Jackie, with toy drum, is talking to Rafael Kubelik

our time playing all over Israel. The audience would be basically women because their sons, husbands and brothers were fighting. There was a special atmosphere in the air and a feeling that it was extremely important to do anything one could through one's abilities as a musician.

I don't actually know why I've been linked so much with the Elgar, unless it's because of its English element. I loved playing it. There is a passage at the end of the concerto which has always meant a great deal to me. It's very inward, very intense, very passionate and flamboyant and at the same time very soft, all of which sounds like a contradiction in terms. It's difficult to play in the sense that one has to be well aware of the kind of sound one is making and know exactly how one wants to achieve this . . .

When I was in Australia I went to a doctor to complain of some symptoms from which I seemed to be suffering and I was told it was adolescent trauma. Not very helpful, although it is not unusual, I believe, for MS to remain undiagnosed in its early stages. I had the frustration and the guilt of thinking: what on earth is wrong? Why am I reacting in this way and feeling lousy at the same time?

It was while I was on my own in America that I had a nightmare of an experience. Rehearsals had been very difficult; I didn't feel in command of the bow. Various areas of my body were numb and I couldn't feel the strings of the cello. I recall arriving at Philharmonic Hall in New York and finding I was unable to open the cello case. I walked onto the platform not knowing how I would find a key or what sounds I was going to produce. I remember then realizing that my only hope was to use my eyes to help my fingers as much as possible. It was not good playing, an indifferent performance. I decided to return home and not fulfil any further engagements. When I got back my illness was quickly diagnosed. Since then I have not given a concert.

When I was told absolutely bluntly that I had MS and that nobody could prophesy what was going to happen, I asked a thousand questions and got straightforward answers. It was perhaps likely that I would not get up from the wheelchair again. It was tough medicine actually, but I was quite grateful, because it meant that for me MS was not shrouded in a great aura of mystery. Since then I have tried to think and work out what I can do from a wheelchair and what I can do is quite a lot.

I was lucky because Daniel was able to stay home at times when he was less busy. Actually he put off many of his engagements so that he could be with me. It is such a big problem when one's movements become restricted before one can find a way of looking after oneself for essentials like food, washing and dressing. At that time, before we had the good fortune to find our very dear housekeeper, Olga, Daniel, who previously hadn't known how to make tea with a tea bag, became very busy in the kitchen studying the rudiments of curry making.

There were long periods of being encompassed by four walls, time to feel very lonely, time to analyse each symptom with great intensity and watch its progress as if under a microscope. Those times were horrible and I managed them very poorly. When things are hard and one is not well, one is very conscious of the effect this has on those who are close to one; of the enormous resources it calls for in them. There is not only the difficulty of trying to learn to face up to the way one must regard oneself, but also finding a way of dealing with the feeling of guilt which such a situation brings upon those who are very close. However willingly it is accepted, it is nevertheless unhappily a part of the whole syndrome.

Maybe I am speaking too soon, but I feel I have gone through the hardest times when it comes to fear and a futile sense of uselessness and hopelessness. I feel that I have experienced all that fully and I hope it is now well behind me. It is a horrid feeling to have to be dependent and it can make one feel absolutely furious at times.

I enjoy listening to music, talking with my friends, going to the park and to concerts. I'm really quite busy. Nothing very special. The norm can be a pleasant if not entirely happy day. There are obviously times when I allow myself to accept the fact that it's normal when one feels low, but it's not the general rule as it was, and I think I can honestly say that I do enjoy very much what I enjoy.

I am not so frightened any more because I know that what I can do and have done in quite bad times, I shall perhaps still be able to do if really bad times come again. I also know that I shall have round me people who are totally steadfast and caring, so that I shall not be left literally alone, as well as perhaps in my own head. I have very good friends. I am very fond of the doctors who look after me and I have a lovely family. Being so surrounded by warmth and affection, I am constantly aware that thousands of people are without these blessings and that the number of those with multiple sclerosis who suffer the additional sorrow of loneliness does not bear contemplation.

When I was preparing *Peter and the Wolf*, Janet Suzman advised me, 'Don't over-emotionalize the words, the music is there to illustrate them.' It occurred to me that this is exactly what I tried to convey to my pupils – that the expression is inbuilt in the music and in the shape of the piece as well. Too much expressive indulgence will distort the musical structure.

Playing my recordings sometimes does give me great pleasure, because it is so much second nature to me that listening to a recording is almost as if I was back there doing it again. Oh, yes, I do find myself wishing I could do it like that now, but it's a great source of comfort and refreshment. I was lucky, you see, because my talent was one which developed very early, so by the time the symptoms of MS developed severely enough to interfere with playing, I had done everything I could have wanted and had had so many marvellous experiences through the cello. So I can't reflect with any bitterness, neither do I have a terrible feeling of remorse. I look back with great pleasure at what I was able to do and the great joy I experienced in doing it.

I was converted to Judaism and Daniel and I wanted our children

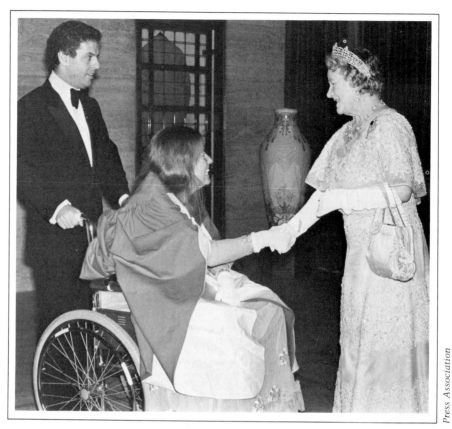

At the University of London Foundation Day dinner the Queen
Mother conferred on Jackie the Honorary Degree of Doctor of
Music, November 1979

brought up in the Jewish faith. But we have no children. I am
sometimes asked if religion has helped me and I always reply – to be
quite honest, not as much as music, because for me the Judaism is
almost bound up in the music. I just cannot separate them or
indicate their boundaries.

I know through all my troubles, I could never say that I am not a
lucky person, because materially and emotionally I am very blessed.
To have the things around which can be so cherished is enough to
make one feel that this is a land full of milk and honey.

Extracts from Jacqueline du Pré's Notebooks

I was always a lover, since childhood, of the winter elements – of snow as it graced the earth gently with its snowflakes leaving that pristine white carpet. Oh, what a shame to spoil its velvet smoothness with a common footprint, but what a delicious excitement to create evidence of one's exploration into a virgin land! I remember the search for the single, magically designed snowflake, or of flinging myself into the snow loving its texture, the cold against one's skin and the fun of constructing hard snowballs to throw at random to watch their passage through the air and then their splintering rebound on the chosen target.

Wind and rain also thrilled me, as the first would dance wildly through my hair, buffeting my cheeks, exciting them to warmth, and also induce beauteous scents, and the second with its patter-patter which would invite the imagination to new worlds, would be the flowers into which I could explore the moisture with my face embedded in them, and the thrill with the luscious scents the rain would invite into my world.

(Written at 2 a.m. when my mind feels somewhat muddy and I have never been much of a mud lover!)

Elgar's photo now hangs on the wall – a document which tells so vividly of his unhappy life. A sick man who had through it a glowing heart in such a profusion of loveliness as expressed in so many of his works. How his face haunts me, and always will.

Never mind about present affliction – any moment may be the next!

I suppose all of us must learn to find independence in dependence.

If the sunshine beckons you, accept its invitation and love the gold quality of it.

A genius is one who, with an innate capacity, affects for good or evil, the life of others.

Don't let the sound of your own wheels drive you crazy.

A relationship is not what you would like it to be – or what you think it is. It defines *itself* by the actual quality of the interchange between the people involved.

Jacqueline du Pré's honours to date

Awarded the OBE   1976

Gained the Suggia Gift   1955

Gold Medal Guildhall School of Music
and Queen's Prize   1960

London début   1961

North American début   1965

Gave first performance of Goehr's Romanza
for Cello and Orchestra, which was written
for her   1968

City of London Midsummer Prize   1975

Fellow of the Guildhall School of Music   1975

Fellow of the Royal College of Music   1976

Incorporated Society of Musicians Medal   1981

Hon. RAM; Hon. Mus.D. London, Open,
Sheffield, Leeds, Salford, Durham

Discography

DVOŘÁK Concerto in B minor, op. 104; *Silent Woods*, op. 68 (Chicago Symphony Orchestra/Barenboim)
UK: ASD 2751   *US*: Ang. S–36046

ELGAR Concerto in E minor, op. 85 (London Symphony Orchestra/Barbirolli); *Sea Pictures*, op. 37; 'Sea Slumber-Song'; 'In Haven' (Capri); 'Sabbath Morning at Sea'; 'Where Corals Lie'; 'The Swimmer' (Dame Janet Baker, London Symphony Orchestra/Barbirolli)
UK: ASD 665 *   *US*: Ang. S–36338

ELGAR Concerto in E minor, op. 85 (London Symphony Orchestra/Barbirolli); DELIUS Cello Concerto (Royal Philharmonic Orchestra/Sargent)   Recorded under the auspices of the Delius Trust
ASD 2764

ELGAR Concerto in E minor, op. 85 (Philadelphia Orchestra/Barenboim)
A concert performance recording
UK: CBS 76529 *   *US*: Col. M–34530

HAYDN Concerto in C major; BOCCHERINI Concerto in B flat major (English Chamber Orchestra/Barenboim)
UK: ASD 2331   *US*: Ang. S–36439

HAYDN Concerto in D major, op. 101; MONN Concerto in G minor (London Symphony Orchestra/Barbirolli)
UK: SXLP 30273 *   *US*: Ang. S–36580

SCHUMANN Concerto in A minor, op. 129; SAINT-SAËNS
Concerto No. 1 in A minor, op. 33 (New Philharmonia/Barenboim)
                    UK: ASD 2498   *US*: Ang. S–36642

Favourite Cello Concertos   HAYDN Concerto in D major, op. 101;
ELGAR Concerto in E minor, op. 85 (London Symphony Orchestra/
Barbirolli); HAYDN Concerto in C major (Hoboken VIIb: 1) (English
Chamber Orchestra/Barenboim); SCHUMANN Concerto in
A minor, op. 129 (New Philharmonia Orchestra/Barenboim);
DVOŘÁK Concerto in B minor, op. 104; *Silent Woods*, op. 68
(Chicago Symphony Orchestra/Barenboim) 3LP set

                                              SLS 895

BRAHMS Sonata No. 1 in E minor, op. 38; Sonata No. 2 in F major,
op. 99. With Daniel Barenboim (piano)
                    UK: ASD 2436   *US*: Ang. S–36544

BEETHOVEN Sonatas No. 1 in F major, op. 5, No. 1; No. 2 in G
minor, op. 5, No. 2; No. 3 in A major, op. 69; No. 4 in C major, op.
102, No. 1; No. 5 in C major, op. 102, No. 2; 7 Variations on 'Bei
Männern' from Mozart's *Die Zauberflöte*; 12 Variations on 'Ein
Mädchen oder Weibchen' from *Die Zauberflöte*, op. 66; 12
Variations on 'See the Conquering Hero Comes' from Handel's
Judas Maccabaeus. With Daniel Barenboim (piano) 3LP set
                    UK: SLS 5042   *US*: 3-Ang. S–3823

BEETHOVEN Trio No. 4 in D, op. 70, no. 1 ('Ghost'). Trio No. 5 in E
flat, op. 70, no. 2. With Daniel Barenboim (piano) and Pinchas
Zukerman (violin).

                                      US: Vox C. 9024

BEETHOVEN Trio No. 6 in B flat major, op. 97 ('Archduke'); Trio
No. 7 in B flat major ('1812'). With Daniel Barenboim (piano) and
Pinchas Zukerman (violin).

                                      ASD 2572 *

BEETHOVEN Piano Trios No. 1–7, no. 14; Trio in E flat (1790/91);
10 Variations on Müller's song 'Ich bin der Schneider Kakadu', op.
121a; 14 Variations in E flat major, op. 44. With Daniel Barenboim
(piano) and Pinchas Zukerman (violin); Clarinet Trio in B flat, op.
11. With Daniel Barenboim (piano) and Gervaise de Peyer (clarinet).
5LP set

                                              SLS 789

A Jacqueline du Pré Recital   VON PARADIS *Sicilienne*; SCHU-
MANN Three Fantasy Pieces, op. 73; MENDELSSOHN Song
Without Words in D, op. 109; FAURÉ Elégie in C minor, op. 24; J. S.
BACH Toccata in C, BWV 564 – Adagio; SAINT-SAËNS *Carnival of
the Animals* – Le Cygne; FALLA *Suite Populaire Espagnole* – Jota;
BRUCH *Kol Nidrei*, op. 47. With Gerald Moore (piano), Roy Jesson
(organ), Osian Ellis (harp) and John Williams (guitar)

HQS 1437

PROKOVIEV Peter and the Wolf, op. 67 (English Chamber
Orchestra/Barenboim). Narrated by Jacqueline du Pré   Recorded
14 October 1979

DG 2531275

* also available on cassette

The Jacqueline du Pré Research Fund for Multiple Sclerosis

It is hoped that the Jacqueline du Pré Research Fund will receive some financial benefit from the sales of this book. For readers wishing to send their own donation the addresses are

The Jacqueline du Pré Research Fund for Multiple Sclerosis
286 Munster Road
London SW6 6AP

The Jacqueline du Pré Research Fund
Multiple Sclerosis Society of Canada
Suite 700
130 Bloor Street West
Toronto
Ontario M5S 1N5
Canada

Jacqueline du Pré Research Fund
International Federation of Multiple Sclerosis Societies
Stubenring 6, A-1010
Vienna
Austria

patient to patient and depend on the site of damage in the myelin sheath and the extent of damage. Millions of people worldwide are believed to have MS, although exact figures are unknown because of the large number of cases that go unreported or await final diagnosis. It is more common in colder climates.

There is, to date, no known cure for multiple sclerosis. Current research focuses on immunology, virology, epidemiology and clinical trials. More than 100 full time investigators based at university medical schools and hospitals are currently pursuing active investigations in both basic and clinical research.

In addition to massive research programs in the United States, Great Britain and Canada, many other Societies support research programs and all member Societies of the Federation provide patient services which include support to MS clinics, medical equipment loans, varied rehabilitative, counseling and recreational programs, and referral services to those who have MS and their families.

Since the inception of the first national Society in the United States, in 1946, more than $69 million has been allocated to research in that country alone. Immense progress has been made in the last decade in understanding the mechanism of the disease. New regimens are now being tested and reported which seem to alter its course.

There is no better way to honor the artistry of Jacqueline du Pré than to join in the battle against multiple sclerosis. If you would like to learn more about the activities and progress in combating multiple sclerosis, or contribute to the Jacqueline du Pré Research Fund, contributions and inquiries can be directed to the Multiple Sclerosis Society at the following address:

Jacqueline du Pré Research Fund
National Multiple Sclerosis Society
205 East 42 Street
New York, N.Y. 10017
Tel. (212) 986–3240   contact: Joan Davis Berger

All royalties from the sale of this book are being donated to the Jacqueline du Pré Research Fund.

George C. Boddiger
Chairman, International
Development Committee
International Federation of
Multiple Sclerosis Societies